Bronze Age Spearheads from Berkshire, Buckinghamshire and Oxfordshire

Margaret R. Ehrenberg

British Archaeological Reports 34
1977

British Archaeological Reports
122 Banbury Road, Oxford OX2 7BP, England

GENERAL EDITORS

A.C.C. Brodribb, M.A.
Mrs. Y.M. Hands

A.R. Hands, B.Sc., M.A., D.Phil.
D.R. Walker, B.A.

ADVISORY EDITORS

C.B. Burgess, M.A.   Neil Cossons, M.A., F.S.A., F.M.A.
Professor B.W. Cunliffe, M.A., Ph.D., F.S.A.
Sonia Chadwick Hawkes, B.A., M.A., F.S.A.
Professor G.D.B. Jones, M.A., D.Phil., F.S.A.
Frances Lynch, M.A., F.S.A.   P.A. Mellars, M.A., Ph.D.
P.A. Rahtz, M.A., F.S.A.

B.A.R. 34, 1977: "Bronze Age Spearheads from Berkshire, Buckinghamshire and Oxfordshire"
© Margaret R. Ehrenberg, 1977

The author's moral rights under the 1988 UK Copyright, Designs and Patents Act are hereby expressly asserted.

All rights reserved. No part of this work may be copied, reproduced, stored, sold, distributed, scanned, saved in any form of digital format or transmitted in any form digitally, without the written permission of the Publisher.

ISBN 9780904531619 paperback
ISBN 9781407319902 e-book
DOI https://doi.org/10.30861/9780904531619
A catalogue record for this book is available from the British Library
This book is available at www.barpublishing.com

CONTENTS

Page

Preface

List of Figures

Introduction 1

Early Bronze Age Spearheads 4

Looped Spearheads 6

Pegged Spearheads 13

Distribution 17

Manufacture, Hafting and Use 20

Chronology and Conclusions 24

Catalogue 27

Appendix I 57

Appendix II 59

Bibliography 61

Figures 67

Plate 95

PREFACE

This study of the bronze spearheads from Berkshire, Buckinghamshire and Oxfordshire was originally submitted as an undergraduate thesis at University College, Cardiff.

The catalogue contains all the spearheads from the three counties known to me, from museums, both within the area and outside, from the Bronze Implements Card Catalogue, the Ordnance Survey record cards, and from relevant published surveys, including the past volumes of the local archaeological journals pertaining to the area. All the material which could be traced was examined, and is described here, and nearly all the spearheads are illustrated. Using the spearheads from the area, various aspects of the bronze spearhead in a wider setting, including their development and chronology, are examined, and the distribution of the spearheads within the area is considered.

I would like to thank all the many people who gave me advice and assistance throughout my work: M. Farley, who suggested the subject to me; all the museum curators and assistants, without whose help this work would not have been possible, including Miss C. M. Johns and Mrs. G. Varndell, British Museum; Mrs. A. Ellison and C. L. Cram, Reading Museum; A. Sherratt, Ashmolean Museum; C. N. Gowing, Buckinghamshire County Museum; Miss J. Macdonald, London Museum; H. H. Coghlan, Borough Museum, Newbury; J. Burr, Windsor Guildhall Exhibition; M. Ballance, Eton College; Miss M. Cra'ster, University Museum of Archaeology and Ethnology, Cambridge and Miss L. Millard, Royal Museum, Canterbury. I am indebted to many of the members of staff and of my fellow-students in the Department of Archaeology at Cardiff, for helpful discussion and advice on numerous points, and especially to Mr. C. B. Burgess, Professor R. J. C. Atkinson and Miss J. Price who read and commented on earlier versions of this paper.

Cardiff
November 1976
Margaret R. Ehrenberg

N.B. In the text spearheads from Berkshire, Buckinghamshire and Oxfordshire are referred to by their provenance, followed by the number in the catalogue, thus:- Reading (98) or (Reading 98).

LIST OF FIGURES

Figure		Page
1	Comparative Table of Spearhead Classifications	3
2	Chronology of Spearhead Types	25
3	Early Bronze Age and Kite Bladed Spearheads (Nos. 86, 45, 3, 98, 2)	69
4	Side-Looped Leaf-Shaped Spearheads (Nos. 89, 120, 9, 129, 27, 56, 5, 103)	70
5	Side-Looped Leaf-Shaped Spearheads (Nos. 93, 57, 4)	71
6	Side-Looped Leaf-Shaped Spearheads (Nos. 101, 61, 11, 59)	72
7	Side-Looped Leaf-Shaped Spearheads (Nos. 91, 28, 90, 48, 104, 92, 80)	73
8	Side-Looped Leaf-Shaped Spearheads (Nos. 143, 140, 146, 24, 43, 69, 62, 63)	74
9	Side-Looped Leaf-Shaped Spearheads (Nos. 25, 26, 108, 65)	75
10	Side-Looped Leaf-Shaped Spearheads (Nos. 71, 10, 58, 35, 7)	76
11	Side-Looped Leaf-Shaped Spearheads (Nos. 68, 64, 100)	77
12	Rapier Bladed Spearhead (No. 121)	78
13	Leaf-Shaped Basal-Looped Spearheads (Nos. 79, 131, 137, 55)	79
14	Leaf-Shaped Basal-Looped Spearheads (Nos. 42, 99, 32, 19, 106)	80
15	Triangular-Bladed Basal-Looped Spearheads (Nos. 139, 133, 54, 47)	81
16	Triangular-Bladed Basal-Looped Spearheads (Nos. 39, 138, 30)	82
17	Triangular-Bladed Basal-Looped Spearheads (Nos. 109, 31, 67, 46, 147, 78)	83
18	Pegged Leaf-Shaped Spearheads (Nos. 37, 38, 123, 97, 122, 75, 111, 113, 124)	84

Figure		Page
19	Pegged Leaf-Shaped Spearheads (Nos. 145, 130, 29, 114, 60, 52)	85
20	Pegged Leaf-Shaped Spearheads (Nos. 115, 112, 116, 96, 117, 44, 12, 33)	86
21	Pegged Leaf-Shaped Spearheads (Nos. 134, 21, 66, 50, 41, 49, 110, 76, 144, 22)	87
22	Pegged Leaf-Shaped Spearheads (Nos. 73, 94, 36, 142, 74, 51, 53, 34, 102)	88
23	Pegged Leaf-Shaped Spearheads (Nos. 132, 17, 20)	89
24	Barbed Spearheads (Nos. 16, 77, 135, 15)	90
25	Barbed Spearheads (Nos. 18, 107, 85)	91
26	Ferrules (Nos. 6, 119, 118, 141)	92
27	The Distribution of Early and Middle Bronze Age Spearheads	93
28	The Distribution of Late Bronze Age Spearheads	94

Plate		
1	Spearhead from Dorchester (54), with Associated Finds	95

INTRODUCTION

Bronze Spearheads

Spearheads are one of the most common Bronze Age metal types, and yet they have received comparatively little attention.

The earliest study of the type was by Wilde (1861) who divided the Irish examples into four classes, which Evans (1881) in <u>Ancient Bronze Implements</u> used as the basis for a detailed discussion of British and Irish spearheads. The only comprehensive work devoted solely to spearheads is a paper by Greenwell and Brewis, published in 1909, in which the typological development of the weapon is discussed, and the classification system still widely used today is proposed. In 1933 E. Evans reviewed several points raised by Greenwell and Brewis.

Since then spearheads have been discussed only in short notes on individual types or in regional surveys of Bronze Age metalwork. Burgess has contributed to the study of Late Bronze Age spearheads, investigating those from northern Britain (1968) and summarizing the main types found throughout the country (1969). Coles (1959-60; 1963-4; 1968-9) has examined the Scottish material and proposed a new system of classification. Britton (1963), Burgess and Cowen (1972) and Gerloff (1975) have studied the Early Bronze Age spearheads, while Smith (1959) has considered those of the Middle Bronze Age in southern Britain. Certain Late Bronze Age types, especially barbed spearheads, have been discussed in some detail by Burgess, Coombs and Davies (1972).

The spearheads fall into several distinct groups which all the classification systems recognize, but describe in different terms. (See Fig. 1.) The classification created by Greenwell and Brewis, which is still often quoted, implies a chronology and relationships between types which no longer seem to be entirely valid, and while a new classification scheme is desirable, this should be based on a comprehensive study of all the bronze spearheads from Britain. Therefore, descriptive terms, as used by Burgess, Smith and others, are preferred here, despite the ambiguity which such terms can sometimes cause, and the following classes are distinguished:

	Blade shape	Attachment to shaft	Midrib cross-section
Tanged	triangular (dagger-like)	tang + rivet hole	slight, usually ovate
End-looped	triangular	loops on socket	arched lozenge
Kite-bladed	kite-shaped	loops on socket	lozenge

	Blade shape	Attachment to shaft	Midrib cross-section
Side-looped	leaf-shaped	loops on socket	usually lozenge, sometimes circular
Basal-looped + leaf-shaped blade	leaf-shaped	loops at base of blade	lozenge
Basal-looped + triangular blade	triangular	loops at base of blade	circular
Rapier-bladed	rapier-shaped	loops on socket	lozenge
Pegged	leaf-shaped	pegholes	circular
Barbed	wide parallel-sided + barbs	pegholes	ovate

The Area

Berkshire, Buckinghamshire and Oxfordshire cover an area of diverse environments, including parts of the Chilterns, the Cotswolds and the Berkshire Downs, but is dominated by the valleys of the river Thames and its tributaries. The width of the Thames and the length over which it was navigable undoubtedly accounts for its great importance at many times in the past, either as a line of communication, or as a north-south barrier. For long periods in the past the light river gravels, extending for an average of about one mile on either side of the river, have attracted extensive settlement (e.g. Benson and Miles 1974). The chalk ridge of the Chilterns and Berkshire Downs links the area with East Anglia on the one hand and Wessex on the other.

	GREENWELL and BREWIS	BURGESS	COLES	SMITH 1959a	COMMENTS	DATE
Tanged	I		A		Tanged	EBA
—	IA				Ferrule added	EBA
End-looped	II Early Socketed	End-looped	B			EBA
Kite-bladed	III	Kite-bladed	C	Socket-looped		MBA
Side-looped	IV	Leaf-shaped.looped	D	Side-looped		MBA
Rapier-bladed	IVA					
—	IVB		F		Protected loop	
Basal-looped with leaf-shaped blade	IIIA	Basal looped with leaf-shaped blade	E	Basal-looped		Ornament Horizon
Basal-looped with triangular blade		Straight based basal looped				Penard phase
Plain Pegged	V					LBA
	VA				Wings on band at sides of midrib	
	VB	Hollow bladed			Hollow bladed	Wilburton
Barbed	VI	Barbed				Broadward Tradition

Fig. 1. Comparative table of Spearhead Classifications.

EARLY BRONZE AGE SPEARHEADS

Bronze spearheads first seem to occur in Britain in the final phase of the Early Bronze Age, when three forms were current, the tanged spearhead of the Arreton tradition, the pegged, early socketed spearhead, possibly also of the Arreton tradition, and the end-looped spearhead of the Inch Island/ Derryniggin tradition.

Tanged Spearheads (Greenwell and Brewis Class I)

Description: Two tanged spearheads (Newbury 86 and Datchet 45) have been found in the area under study; these are characterized by a thin triangular blade with an ovate midrib, which is defined by one or more grooves or steps and a tang with a small rivethole at the base of the blade.

Distribution and Chronology: Tanged spearheads are one of the earliest forms of bronze spearhead in Britain, probably deriving from the bronze daggers of the Camerton-Snowshill type, which have the same blade shape and moulding as the spearhead; a tang, more suitable for hafting the shaft of a spear, replaces the butt of the dagger. Gerloff (1975, 252) lists 38 examples, found widely scattered over most of England and including five hoards (Arreton Down, I.o.W; Plymstock, Devon; Totland, I.o.W; Stoke Abbott, Dorset; Buckland, Dover, Kent). These associate the spearheads with types belonging to the Arreton tradition of the later Early Bronze Age, such as flanged axes of the Arreton type and Camerton-Snowshill daggers.

End-looped Spearheads (Class II)

Description: End-looped spearheads (Burgess and Cowen, 1972) or Class II, early socketed spearheads (Greenwell and Brewis, 1909), which have a socket extending as far as the base of the blade, which is triangular or diamond shaped, and divided from it by the curving or V-shaped line of the base of the blade moulding; the type may either have pegholes to secure it to its shaft, or loops which are characteristically very near to the mouth of the socket. The spearhead from Akeley (3) is a looped example, typical in its moulding of the blade, the loops and the incised and pointillé decoration, and is particularly closely paralleled by one from Dean Water, Angus (Coles, 1968-9, 4).

Distribution and Chronology: Five of the pegged type have been found in south and east England and one is known from Scotland (Gerloff, 1975, 254); the looped version, or end-looped spearhead, is relatively common in Ireland but only eight are known from England and Wales (Burgess and Cowen, 1972, 172). A pegged example in the Arreton hoard, and an end-looped spearhead in the Ebnal, Shropshire, hoard, associated with two Camerton-Snowshill daggers and an Arreton-type flanged axe imply that the two types were broadly contemporary in the final phase of the Early Bronze Age. However, the distribution of the end-looped spearheads suggests that they belong to the Irish Inch Island/Derryniggin tradition. Also, from the distribution of early spearhead types with loops on the socket, it seems plausible that loops were an Irish innovation, though the record of associated finds suggests that they became the exclusive method of spearhead attachment in Britain until the Penard phase. Imports of these and the slightly later kite-bladed spearheads in Britain may have been the prototypes for the British side-looped spearheads, and may, perhaps, have been one of the causes of the demise of the pegged variant.

LOOPED SPEARHEADS

There were three main types of spearhead current in the Middle Bronze Age; besides the basal-looped spearhead there were two smaller forms with loops on the sides of the socket, which are clearly distinguishable by the shape of the blade. Those with kite-shaped blades form Greenwell and Brewis Class III, and Smith's (1959a, 180) socket-looped group, while Greenwell and Brewis Class IV, Smith's side-looped spearhead, have leaf-shaped blades. The distribution of the two types offers a contrast: kite-bladed spearheads are common in Ireland, but rare in Britain, whereas side-looped leaf-shaped spearheads occur throughout Britain but are less common in Ireland (Coles, 1963-4, 106; Eogan, 1964. 268). This contrast is clear in the area under study, where two kite-shaped spearheads and over 40 side-looped spearheads have been found.

Kite-Bladed Spearheads (Class III)

Description: These weapons are characterized by a kite-shaped blade which often has either ribs or grooves converging on the midrib and may have a rib running along the top of the midrib, which ends about half-way up the blade. They have a pair of loops which are lozenge-shaped in side view and are placed on the socket approximately midway between the base of the blade and the mouth of the socket. Reading (98) is a fairly typical example with a rib on the blade only. Sparsholt (104) falls typologically between this type and side-looped spearheads; its wide blade can be compared either with kite-shaped blades, or with ivy-leafed blades, such as on the looped spearhead from Millbourne, Northumberland (Cowen, 1966, 234). The decoration of the Sparsholt spearhead is more commonly found on kite-bladed spearheads from Ireland than on side-looped spearheads. On the other hand its rounded midrib is more usual on leaf-shaped spearheads. Akeley (2) is also somewhat anomalous, possessing features which link it both with kite-bladed and leaf-shaped looped spearheads.

Distribution: The overall distribution of kite-bladed spearheads, with the vast majority found in Ireland and a thin scatter in Britain, suggests that they may be the product of an Irish industrial tradition, probably developing from the end-looped spearhead (Coles, 1963-4, 104).

Chronology: The typological similarity of this class to end-looped spearheads, and the occurrence on some examples of 'rain pattern' and other decoration, more commonly found on Early Bronze Age axes, daggers and spearheads, suggests that the type began early in the Middle Bronze Age. This is confirmed by the evidence of a small number of associated finds and moulds, especially one from Killymaddy, Co. Antrim (Coghlan and Raftery, 1961, 232) which has matrices both for group II dirks, which seem to have come into use during the Acton Park phase of the Middle Bronze Age

(Burgess, 1968b, 12), and for kite-bladed spearheads. Two associations with Late Bronze Age metal types may imply that the type was long-lived (Coles, 1963-4, 104).

Side-Looped Spearheads (Class IV)

Description: Side-looped leaf-shaped spearheads vary considerably in size, but examples are generally smaller than basal-looped spearheads with which they are roughly contemporary. The examples from the area under study range from 90-210 mm; few are over 160 mm and almost half are less than 120 mm.

The loops, used for attaching the head to the shaft, are either string loops or lozenge-shaped, or a hybrid of the two, that is, narrow loops with semi-circular profile, slightly flattened by hammering (e.g. Aylesbury 11). The eye i.e. the internal diameter, of the loops on this type of spearhead, is almost always very small, particularly in the string-looped examples, the maximum dimensions noted in the area being 3 x 1.5 mm. Therefore it would probably have been difficult to secure the shaft of a side-looped spearhead as firmly as the shaft of a basal-looped spearhead (these have stronger loops, with larger eyes) unless a much shorter and lighter shaft were used. This may indicate different functions for the two types. Alternatively, the evidence of a smaller number of examples in which the eyes of the loops have not been made, presumably owing to faulty casting e.g. Fyfield (61) or Standlake (108) might suggest that the small loops were non-functional and the shaft was only wedged into the socket, or that the loops had a function other than for securing the shaft. In most cases the loops were placed approximately half-way between the base of the blade and the mouth of the socket, although a few examples from the area have their loops placed close to the base of the blade, e.g. Burghfield (26).

The blade. The term 'leaf-shaped' may be applied to the majority of blades, although within this term a variety of shapes are included. Some examples have the maximum width of the blade near its centre e.g. Newbury (88), whereas on others the maximum width is low down on the blade, e.g. Eton (57). Some side-looped spearheads have ogival blades, which may be due to the original shape of the mould, or to subsequent sharpening, e.g. Kintbury (71), Eton (58). This shape, more usual on pegged spearheads, is also found on a side-looped leaf-shaped spearhead from Middle Gussage, Dorset (Moore and Rowlands, 1972, 59), there considered to be caused by resharpening, or at Osgoodby, Lincs (Davey, 1973, 79). Some of the blades have bevelled edges.

The section of the midrib of side-looped spearheads is either circular, or more usually lozenge-shaped, becoming round below the blade. Two examples from Windsor (140 and 143) have a ridge running along the top of the midrib, from the tip, where it merges into the lozenge-shape of the midrib, and continuing almost to the socket mouth. Such a rib is typical of, and may be a borrowing from, kite-bladed spearheads, although it can be paralleled on other leaf-shaped examples e.g. from Nethermuir, Aberdeen (Coles, 1963-4, 105).

The socket extends internally between 40% and 70% of the total length of the spearhead, usually continuing into the blade for a short distance.

Decoration: A few of the spearheads are decorated. Aston (10) and Pusey (93) have a groove above the mouth of the socket, below which the socket is slightly expanded, and Shifford (101) and Burghfield (28) have punched triangular notches around the mouth of the socket; both these features may have been made after the shaft had been fitted and primarily intended to fasten the head more firmly to the shaft. Pusey (93) also has pointillé decoration.

Many different combinations of loop, blade and midrib type occur, but more work over the country as a whole is needed to understand the regional and chronological significance of these.

Distribution: Side-looped spearheads occur throughout the country but are concentrated in North Wiltshire, Berkshire, Oxfordshire and the Thames valley (Moore and Rowlands, 1972, 19).

Origin: The precise origin of the side-looped leaf-shaped spearhead is unclear. The blade shape is thought to have derived from the continent, where spearheads with leaf-shaped blade and pegholes were usual throughout the Middle Bronze Age (Smith, 1959, 180), although few continental Middle Bronze Age spearheads have been recognized in Britain. Smith also suggests that the type developed early in the Middle Bronze Age at the same time as the kite-bladed spearhead in Ireland which implies that the loops either derived from the very small number of end-looped spearheads in Britain, or were independently invented. Alternatively, the type may have been developed at a slightly later date, either in Britain or in Ireland, from kite-bladed spearheads, some of which are typologically similar to, or transitional to side-looped spearheads e.g. Akeley (2). (cf. Rowlands, 1976, 51.)

Chronology: The development of the type may either have taken place in the Acton Park phase of the Middle Bronze Age or during the Ornament Horizon; although side-looped spearheads are not attested until the Ornament Horizon, this need not be taken to conclusively indicate that they were not being produced earlier since the number of hoards of the Acton Park phase is extremely small (Burgess, 1974, 313).

It is perhaps more likely, however, that the type was first produced in the Ornament Horizon, where it is attested in hoards and on settlement sites. Small string-looped examples are best attested in true Ornament Horizon hoards, such as the Monkswood hoard (Smith, 1959b, GB 42) and the Stump Bottom hoard (Smith, 1959a, 153), and also on Deverel-Rimbury settlement sites such as Thorny Down (Hawkes, 1941, 130). In addition to two side-looped spearheads, the Burgesses Meadow hoard (24 and 25) contains a low-flanged palstave, a flat tanged knife, a chisel and a socketed hammer. The last of these is made of leaded bronze, which on the evidence of southern British analyses suggests a Late Bronze Age date, although recent analyses (Northover, unpublished research) have shown that leaded bronze was used in Wales in the Middle Bronze Age, so that the occurrence of lead can no longer be used as a firm indicator of the Late Bronze Age.

Some side-looped spearheads, particularly the larger ones with flattened loops, probably continued to be used and manufactured after the Ornament Horizon, as they occur in more late Middle Bronze Age and Late Bronze Age contexts than would seem likely if they were merely residual pieces. They occur, for example, in the Inshoch Wood, Nairn hoard with a socketed hammer and an anvil, which is best paralleled in the Bishopsland hoard (Coles, 1968-9, 19) probably contemporary with the Penard phase (Burgess, 1969, 4) and in the Shelf, Yorks. hoard with transitional and late palstaves (Burgess, 1968, 62), and in the Fell Lane, Penrith hoard with a Yorkshire socketed axe characteristic of the Heathery Burn tradition (Burgess, 1968, 21). Two occur in the Yattendon hoard (Y37 and Y40). In addition to the evidence from hoards, two side-looped spearheads analysed by Brown and Blin-Stoyle (1959, 196), one from Methwold, Cambs. and one from Fyfield, Berks (61) were made of leaded bronze, which in Southern Britain was probably uncommon before the Wilburton phase (but see above). A mould from Aberdeenshire (Coles, 1963-4, 106) was used for making both leaf-shaped spearheads and leaf-shaped pegged spearheads.

There is one radio-carbon date for a side-looped spearhead from Tormarton, Glos.: bone from the skeleton in which two of these spearheads were lodged gave a date of 977 ± 90 b.c. (c. 1100 B.C.), which on the latest chronology puts it into the Penard phase (Burgess, 1976, 74).

Rapier-Bladed Spearheads (Class IVA)

Description: The blade of the spearhead from Taplow (121) obviously copies the shape of a rapier, being wide at the base and narrowing sharply after a few centimetres, and it has two studs on each face of the "butt", which are either made of gold or may be covered with gold foil. The spearhead has loops on the socket, placed near to the base of the blade, and is decorated with pointillé and incised decoration.

Distribution and Chronology: This example belongs to a small group of rapier-bladed spearheads; Evans (1933, 194) knew of only six in Ireland and two or three in England. There is no evidence for the chronological position of the group, but the apparent hybridisation of basal- or side-looped spearheads and rapiers of Burgess's group I-III (1968b, 3) i.e. those with trapeze-shaped butt and narrow blade points to a date in the Middle Bronze Age, before the Penard phase.

Basal-Looped Spearheads (Class IIIA)

An important group of spearheads has loops at the base, and forming part, of the blade. Two quite distinct types of basal-looped spearhead can be recognized in the British series, those with leaf-shaped blades, which belong to the middle of the Middle Bronze Age, and those with triangular blades, of the later part of the Middle Bronze Age. The blade shape is not the only criterion which distinguishes the two varieties. Those with leaf-shaped blades have lozenge-shaped loops, and the cross-section of the midrib is invariably lozenge-shaped, whereas basal-looped spearheads with triangular blades have loops which are narrow, and have circular cross-section midribs.

Basal-Looped Spearheads with Leaf-Shaped Blades

Description: Thirteen examples of the type have been found in Berkshire, Buckinghamshire and Oxfordshire, most of which are about 240 mm long. Although there is some variation in the shape of the blade, the leaf-shaped blades of this group have their maximum width three-quarters to half-way between the tip and the base of the blade. The midrib is always lozenge-sectioned, becoming circular at, or just below, the base of the blade. Marlow (79) has a narrow rib running along the top of the midrib. This seems to be relatively common over the country as a whole and may be an early feature, as it is commonly found on kite-bladed spearheads and is paralleled, for example, on a basal-looped spearhead from Leisbuttel, Netherlands (Butler, 1963, 100) in an association which has been assigned to Montelius IIb/c, and also in the Stibbard hoard (Britton, 1960, GB 50). On either side of the midrib is a channel running along the length of the blade. The loops are formed as continuations of the edges of the blade and are always wider than the maximum thickness of the wings, varying from leaf-shaped to angular lozenge-shaped.

Origin: The origin of the basal-looped spearhead is far from clear, although it has been discussed on a number of occasions (Evans, 1881, 327; Coffey, 1896, 498; Greenwell and Brewis, 1909, 461; Evans, 1933, 91; Rowlands, 1976, 57). Rowlands suggests that the type originated in Ireland, where these spearheads are certainly more varied in form than the British series, which may imply that they are earlier and in a more experimental stage. It may be that basal loops were found to be easier to manufacture, or stronger, and therefore more suited to a particular function, perhaps a different one from the side-looped spearheads (see above, page 7).

Chronology: Leaf-shaped basal-looped spearheads have a wide distribution in Britain and Ireland (Evans, 1933, 193). An export of the type to the continent, from Leisbuttel, in the Netherlands, with Montelius IIb/c associations suggests that the type was being produced in the Ornament Horizon. In Britain the few associations which include basal-looped spearheads with leaf-shaped blades show that they are typical of the Ornament Horizon; examples are found in ornament hoards or with south-western palstaves (Smith, 1959a, 47) such as the Taunton Workhouse hoard (Smith, 1959b, GB 43) and in the Sherford hoard (Smith, 1959b, GB 45). While nearly all finds are in Ornament Horizon hoards, it seems likely, in view of their much wider distribution as stray finds, that these hoards have drawn on a widespread and possibly older native tradition (Smith, 1959a, 179). An example of the type exported to the continent was found at Weisloch near Heidelberg, in association with a Rixheim sword and Ha A1 pottery and can therefore be equated with the earliest stages of the Penard phase. Another of these weapons from Speen (106 and 107) was associated with a barbed spearhead of the Ewart Park phase. However, production seems to have ceased by the later Middle Bronze Age, Penard phase, the type giving way to triangular bladed basal-looped and pegged weapons. Although more hoards occur in succeeding phases, so far as I am aware, only the Weisloch and Speen hoards contain leaf-shaped basal-looped spearheads.

Basal-Looped Spearheads with Triangular Blades

Description: There are eleven examples of the type from the area; they vary considerably in size, tending to be longer than any other class of Bronze Age spearhead, ranging from 120 mm to 470 mm.

The shape of the blade varies less than other forms, although, as Coles (1963-4, 106) has noticed of Scottish examples, 'spearheads with distinctly triangular blades are limited, while others show a progression from the leaf-shaped blade. In these the line of the blade base still curves more or less at right angles to the socket, but the angle of the blade-edge and blade base is not acute but rounded.' The same is true of the examples from Berkshire, Buckinghamshire and Oxfordshire. Old Windsor (138) and Cookham (39), for example, have blades with right angled bases, while Walingford (133) and Statfield Mortimer (109) have rounded edges, but in every other feature are typical of the class.

The loops of triangular-bladed basal-looped spearheads are always narrow, and are usually the same width as the maximum width of the wings. Sometimes they join the socket at an obtuse angle, e.g. Caversham (30), as is usual on leaf-shaped basal-looped spearheads, or at right angles. e.g. Cookham (39) or Maidenhead (78). Both types can be readily paralleled by similar examples from many parts of the country. A few spearheads, for example, Cookham (39) have pegholes as well as basal loops. This feature is occasionally found elsewhere, as on the spearhead from Pyotdykes, Angus (Coles, 1964, 191) or on another from the Thames at Teddington (Greenwell and Brewis, 1909, Pl. LXIII). These holes were perhaps made at some time subsequent to the manufacture of the spearhead and may be indicative of the continued use of the type in the Late Bronze Age; the Pyotdykes example, which has Ewart Park associations, helps to strengthen this hypothesis.

Origin: The type can be seen as an indigenous development from leaf-shaped basal-looped spearheads and is one of a number of changes in metal types occurring in the Penard phase. The main concentrations of triangular bladed basal-looped spearheads are in the river Thames, the Fens and in Ireland (Burgess, Coombs and Davies, 1972, 225), closely following the distribution of other Penard types (Burgess, 1969, 4).

Chronology: A number of associated finds show that these weapons are typical of the Penard, or final phase of the Middle Bronze Age. The Appleby, Lincs. hoard (Davey and Knowles, 1971, 154) contains three examples as well as a number of rapiers and a sword all of which belong to the Penard phase. Other examples occur in the Ambleside hoard (Coles, 1965, 43), the Shelf hoard (Burgess, 1968, 10) and the Maentwrog hoard (Hawkes and Smith, 1955, GB 10), and in North-West France the type occurs in hoards of the Rosnoën phase, contemporary with the Penard phase in Britain. There are no associations which would suggest that the type began before the Penard phase, but in Northern Britain the type is found in Wallington hoards and its continued use later in the Late Bronze Age is attested in the Pyotdykes hoard (see above) and in the Kish, Co. Wicklow hoard of the Dowris phase, which is contemporary with the Ewart Park phase (Eogan, 1964, 350).

The Yattendon hoard also supports the continued use of the type into the Late Bronze Age; as well as one of these spearheads, it contains a number of earlier metal types, and has a terminus post quem in the Ewart Park phase for the deposition of the hoard.

PEGGED SPEARHEADS

Plain Pegged Spearheads (Class V)

By far the most common and widespread form of spearhead in the Late Bronze Age is Greenwell and Brewis Class V, which has a simple leaf-shaped or ogival blade and pegholes on the socket for securing the shaft, but there is a great deal of variation within the group.

Description: The size of the spearheads varies considerably, from under 100 mm to over 400 mm, most being between 100 and 200 mm. The pegholes, which are set opposite each other, are usually placed about half-way between the mouth of the socket and the base of the blade, and are 3-6 mm in diameter.

The blade. Most pegged spearheads have blades which are either lanceolate leaf-shaped, elliptical leaf-shaped or ogival (Burgess, Coombs and Davies, 1972, 214), and which accounts for about three-quarters of the total length of the spearhead.

The socket, which in most cases has a circular internal and external cross-section usually extends between half- and three-quarters of the total length of the spearhead. A few pegged spearheads are decorated with series of incised lines around the mouth of the socket.

Origin: Pegholes were first used in Britain as a means of spearhead hafting in the later part of the Early Bronze Age on early socketed weapons. Subsequently they seem to have gone out of favour in Britain, but remained the only form of spearhead attachment throughout the Middle Bronze Age on the continent. They were probably reintroduced into Britain in the Penard phase, along with other continental types, such as the first leaf-shaped swords and pointed ferrules (Burgess, 1968, 5), although it is possible that some Middle Bronze Age pegged spearheads occur in Britain, as yet undetected from the mass of Late Bronze Age examples.

Chronology: There are a few associations which show that pegged spearheads occurred in the Penard phase, although they may not have been very common. These include two in the recently discovered Dover hoard (Coombs, 1975, 194), a Ballintober sword with a spearhead in the Worth, Devon hoard (Tucker, 1867, 120) and the Penard hoard itself, with a bronze arrowhead, a Ballintober sword and other typical Penard artefacts (Wheeler, 1921, 138). The Penard spearheads seem to have the most symmetrical blades, with the maximum width near the middle of the blade, and a fairly narrow socket (Burgess, 1969, figs. 3 and 5). Reading (97) might, perhaps, be assigned to this early period.

Pegged spearheads continued to be used throughout the Late Bronze Age. Some sub-types can be distinguished, and those which occur in Berkshire,

Buckinghamshire and Oxfordshire are discussed below. However, the majority of pegged spearheads of simple leaf-shaped blade form cannot at present be assigned to any particular phase of the Late Bronze Age. They occur in hoards of all periods, for example, in the Wilburton or late-Wilburton hoard from Guilsfield, Montgomery (Davies, 1967), in the Broadward tradition hoard from Yattendon, Berks. and in the very late Bronze Age hoard from Welby, Leics. (Powell, 1948, 30).

Wilburton types

The numerous hoards of the Wilburton tradition of southern England contain a variety of characteristic but rare types such as the stepped bladed spearhead (Burgess, 1969, 36) like Reading (96) or Taplow (117). Hollow bladed spearheads, i.e. those where the internal cross-section of the socket in its upper portion follows the profile of the blade, such as Reading (96) or Clewer (33) have parallels in the Guilsfield hoard (Davies, 1967, 98). Windsor (145) and Tilehurst (130), spearheads with offset blades i.e. where the base of the blade does not merge smoothly into the socket but ends abruptly (Coombs, 1975, 60), as well as spearheads with lozenge cross-sectioned blades such as Datchet (44) or Benson (12) are also paralleled in the Guilsfield hoard, and in other Wilburton phase hoards.

Spearhead with Tear-drop blade

Cookham (34) has a wide tear-drop shaped blade, apparently more characteristic of the northern Wallington tradition, contemporary with the Wilburton tradition in the south, and which Coles (1963-4, 110) suggests may have been influenced by triangular-bladed basal-looped spearheads. Tear-drop blades often occur combined with protected openings, such as the examples from Malham, Yorks., Ripon area, Yorks., and Snape, Yorks. (Burgess, 1968, 20) and on spearheads of Montelius IV and V in northern Europe.

Spearheads with Openings in the blade

No spearheads with lunate openings in the blade have been found in the area, but two spearheads, both from Bray (17 and 20), which have large perforations in the blade, may be variants of this type. Spearheads with similar, but not identical perforations have been found in Britain for example, at Denhead, Angus (Evans, 1881, 337) and at Ovington, Northumberland (Burgess, 1968, 33). An example from France (BM 1920, fig. 130) has an hexagonal socket similar to Bray (20). None of this type have been found in hoards, but on typological grounds they may be contemporary with, or slightly later than, spearheads with lunate openings found in Wilburton and later contexts, (Davies, 1967, 101) for example in the Guilsfield hoard.

Spearheads with Ogival blades

Some pegged spearheads e.g. Headington (66) and Bray (22), have a markedly ogival blade. Parallels to these are found in, and seem characteristic of, hoards of the Carp's Tongue Complex of the later part of the Late Bronze Age in South-East England. There are examples in the Thorndon, Suffolk hoard (Hawkes and Snith, 1955, GB 11) associated with a socketed knife, a gouge and a hammer and in the Eaton, Norwich hoard (Langmaid, 1966, fig. 6j) associated with a bugle-shaped object, tanged chisels, a bag-shaped chape and a flesh-hook. These ogival spearheads are frequently decorated, almost invariably with linear or geometric, punched or incised, simple encircling grooves, of which Bray (22) or Maidenhead (76) are typical.

Short Stumpy Spearheads

These spearheads are usually less than 100 mm in length, and the maximum width of the blade is about one third of the length of the weapon. The socket mouth is comparatively large and the socket extends internally almost as far as the tip of the spearhead. Pusey (94) is a good example from the area. In the Waterden, Norfolk hoard an example is associated with a Ewart Park sword, (Langmaid, 1966, 31) and in the Meldreth, Cambs. hoard (Hawkes and Smith, 1955, GB 13) with socketed axes, a Ewart Park sword and a bucket paralleled at Heathery Burn. The type seems, therefore, to be characteristic of the Ewart Park phase of the Late Bronze Age.

Sonning (102)

This spearhead does not seem to have any parallels made of bronze in Britain. Its thin solid blade and long narrow socket have a fairly close analogue in the iron spearhead from the Llyn Fawr, Glam. hoard (Crawford and Wheeler, 1921, 134). A rather longer example, also of iron, comes from the cemetery at Court-St-Etienne in France (Marien, 1958, 110). The cast decoration around the socket is similar, but not identical to an example in the Broadward hoard (Burgess, 1969, 24 fig. 3a) and probably to the spearhead from Wallingford (136) which was associated with late Bronze Age/early Iron Age pottery (see Appendix II). This example may, therefore, have been made late in the Bronze Age or early in the Iron Age, while bronze was still in common use, as a copy of an imported Hallstatt iron spearhead.

Barbed Spearheads (Class VI)

Burgess, Coombs and Davies (1972) have divided barbed spearheads into four groups i-iv, of which examples of groups i and ii occur in Berkshire, Buckinghamshire and Oxfordshire.

Description: The single example of type i from Moulsford (85) has an almost leaf-shaped, lozenge-sectioned blade and very small barbs.

The six group ii examples from the area are all very similar, being between 230 mm and 270 mm long and 60-70 mm wide, and are particularly heavy, most being over 300 g. The blade is parallel-sided or slightly convex almost as far as the tip, where it curves in sharply to a point, and has barbs extending about an extra 15 mm towards the socket. The narrow midrib is ovate in section and defined by a slight step. Just below the barbs are a pair of peg-holes in line with the wings, which are larger than most of the peg-holes of plain pegged spearheads. In four examples a distinctive bronze peg remains in situ. As these pegs are 50-60 mm long they extend beyond the sides of the socket as far as the points of the barbs, and are 7-9 mm in diameter. Both ends are rounded, and where it was possible to examine them, the centre of the peg was cut away, forming a bar with rectangle cross-section inside the shaft. Where it is possible to tell, the socket is either particularly short or is blocked by the remains of a clay core, so that the shaft would scarcely have been able to support the weight of the head.

Origin and Distribution: Barbed spearheads may have developed as an insular phenomenon from the hollow-bladed spearhead of the Willburton tradition and the triangular bladed spearhead, which, if the loops were broken, would have looked similar to the barb and projecting pin of the barbed spearhead (Burgess, Coombs and Davies, 1972, 224). The distribution of the type shows a dense concentration on the Thames Valley, with a few outliers in other parts of southern Britain (Burgess, 1969, 25).

Chronology: The chronological position of these spearheads seems fairly secure. None are found in any late Wilburton hoards, although they frequently occur in hoards such as the Yattendon hoard where the Wilburton element is still strong, but where there are also a number of Carp's Tongue pieces. They also occur in a number of very distinctive hoards, marked especially by the presence of these spearheads, such as the Broadness, Kent or the Broadward, Shrops. hoards, the latter giving rise to the name Broadward tradition for the group of hoards. Burgess, Coombs and Davies (1972, 226) suggest that the "Broadward smiths" of the Middle Thames began production at the very end of the Wilburton phase and moved north and west in the face of oncoming movements by the owners of the Carp's Tongue material in south and east England, probably in the eighth century, and at the same time as the Wilburton tradition spread the idea of using lead-bronze and the Ewart Park sword.

Ferrules or Butts

Only four ferrules have been found in Berkshire, Buckinghamshire and Oxfordshire, all of which are of the simple tubular form. Three are cylindrical, of which one is closed at one end, while the other two are open at both ends. In the case of Taplow (119) this may be due to its having been broken off. The fourth ferrule, from Amerden (6) is of slightly conical form with a closed rounded base. The diameter of the three cylindrical ones is about 10 mm, noticeably less than the average diameter of the socket of pegged spearheads with which they are contemporary. The shaft would, therefore, have had to have been tapered to fit into the ferrule.

The purpose of the ferrule which was fitted onto the far end of the shaft and sometimes secured by a peg or rivet, e.g. the two examples from Taplow, was probably partly to balance the weight of the spear and partly to prevent the bottom of the shaft from splitting.

The ferrule seems to have been introduced into Britain from central Germany in the Penard phase; the long tubular form, either tapering slightly, and evenly, from the mouth to the either flat or rounded closed base, or with a slightly thickened middle such as all the four from the area, is dominant in southern Britain in the Wilburton phase (Burgess, Coombs and Davies, 1972, 216).

DISTRIBUTION

The recorded distribution of spearheads within Berkshire, Buckinghamshire and Oxfordshire may be very different from the true distribution of all spearheads lost or deposited there during the Bronze Age. More than two-thirds of the spearheads from the area come from the rivers Thames and Kennet, and the interpretation of riverine distributions poses special problems.

Nearly all the material from the Thames was found during dredging by the Thames Conservancy Board, which is carried out primarily to keep the river navigable. In the past most of its work has taken place in the lower reaches of the river, particularly below Taplow, which might help to explain the concentrations further downstream. The Thames Conservancy Board takes care to record the provenance of artefacts, but until recently this record was related only to the nearest town, bridge or lock and therefore all the material from a stretch of river several miles long may have been assigned to one find-spot. Most of the towns along the Thames have grown up at easy bridging or fording points, so objects said to have come from these towns have been used, in the past, to suggest that early settlement or activity took place on the same site, but while it is quite likely that early man also chose naturally advantageous positions for his settlements the evidence of material dredged from the Thames cannot be used to prove it.

Another factor to be taken into account is the extent to which an object deposited in the river will be moved by river currents. If a spear with its shaft is dropped into the river, it will almost certainly float until either the shaft breaks or it becomes waterlogged. The good condition of the weapons suggests that once a spearhead has sunk it will rapidly become embedded in the mud and silt of the river bed and protected from disturbance and river movement.

The very small number of Early Bronze Age spearheads from the area makes the significance of their distribution (Fig. 27) impossible to interpret.

Clearer distribution patterns begin to emerge when considering the Middle Bronze Age spearheads (Fig. 27) although the amount of material is still comparatively small. The distribution of side-looped spearheads contrasts with that of basal-looped spearheads. Side-looped spearheads are fairly widely distributed in the southern part of the area with a significant number of finds away from the river Thames. There is a concentration on either side of the river in the Upper Thames basin above Oxford, a spread along the Kennett valley and a small group in the Chilterns. A concentration of side-looped spearheads from the Thames below Taplow is in accord with the dense concentration of all the bronze spearhead types in that area. By contrast, almost all the basal-looped spearheads come either from the Thames or from provenances very close to the river. The leaf-shaped basal-looped spearheads are sparsely distributed along the Kennet and the Thames below Reading, and there are two examples in the Yattendon hoard, as well as two from land sites, both in the Upper Thames basin. Triangular-bladed basal-looped spearheads are scattered at intervals along the Thames downstream from Oxford.

Spearheads of Late Bronze Age type (Fig. 28) show an even more markedly riverine distribution; only in the Yattendon hoard and the Mollington hoard were spearheads found more than two miles from the Thames or Kennet, and almost all the others come from the rivers or close to the banks. All but two of the barbed spearheads come from below Marlow, being a continuation of the main concentration of the type in the Lower Thames (Burgess, Coombs and Davies, 1972, 225). The intensity of concentration of pegged spearheads below Marlow is also particularly noticeable.

It is clear from the distribution of spearheads in the area under study that the river Thames, particularly below Marlow was of prime importance throughout the Bronze Age. But it is important to note that this distribution does not correlate with that of all Bronze Age metal types. An examination of the Bronze Implements Card Catalogue in the British Museum has shown that the predominantly riverine distribution of spearheads correlates closely with that of swords, but that it is quite different from the distribution of tools which occur much more widely throughout the area. A recent survey of the metalwork from Lincolnshire (Davey, 1971, 103) has shown the same two-fold distribution. However, side-looped spearheads are an exception, corresponding with the distribution pattern of tools.

A number of explanations have been put forward for the discovery of Bronze Age weapons in rivers.

Some of the objects could have been lost out of boats as either immigrants, invaders or traders travelled on the river, or at fords by people crossing the Thames. Neither, however, accounts satisfactorily for the completely disproportionate number of weapon finds from the river.

Some of the weapons may have come from hoards of metalwork buried in the river banks, or from settlement sites established by the river, which have been deposited into the river as the banks have been eroded. The amount of erosion known to have occurred over the past century suggests that over several thousand years the course of the river has changed considerably, so that any material which was originally close to the river bank would almost certainly have been eroded into the river. The amount of material of all periods from the Neolithic to the present day which has been dredged from the river might support the theory of erosion. At Wallingford (see Appendix II) a Late Bronze Age/Early Iron Age site, was observed as it was being eroded into the river, and the well-known site at Old England, Brentford (Wheeler, 1929, 20) may be a similar case.

However, perhaps the most likely explanation for most of the metalwork which has been dredged from the river is that during the Bronze Age the river had ritual significance and that various artefacts were thrown in as votive offerings (e.g. Burgess, Coombs and Davies, 1972, 228), or as part of a burial ritual (Jope, 1961, 32); this would have been a precursor to the same ritual known from the Celtic world, which is evidenced by the Battersea and Witham shields and the finds from Llyn Cerrig Bach, and could explain the far greater percentage of weapons than tools and of larger spearheads, e.g. basal-looped, than smaller ones such as side-looped spearheads found in the river, and perhaps also the greater concentration of finds below Marlow, where the river becomes wider and more impressive.

MANUFACTURE, HAFTING AND USE

Manufacture

Nearly all bronze spearheads were cast in two-piece moulds. A number of these have survived, mainly in Ireland and the highland zone of Britain.

The moulds for Early and Middle Bronze Age artefacts are nearly all of stone, usually steatite, which is soft and easily worked. In the Late Bronze Age clay moulds became common in the highland zone; in southern Britain the absence of any moulds in the Middle, and few in the Late Bronze Age may suggest that clay moulds were used; these are more friable, and therefore less likely to be discovered as stray finds. The clay moulds may have been made using a wooden pattern, examples of which have been found in Ireland (Hodges, 1954, 122). In the Middle and Late Bronze Age, bronze moulds were used for casting palstaves and axes, but no spearhead moulds of bronze have been found.

The two pieces of the mould were either tied together or located by dowel pegs. The core, for producing the hollow socket of the spearhead, had to be held in position; in the Late Bronze Age, pegs, or bars, joined the main pieces of the mould to the core and at the same time held the core in place and produced the pegholes (Tylecote, 1962, 122). In some moulds, into which the metal must have been poured from the tip of the spearhead, the core would have been located securely at the base. Most moulds must have been filled from the socket end, the core being fixed in place by chaplets, or trunnions, or the core and the sprue cup into which the metal is poured, might have been made in one piece.

The metal used during the Bronze Age was an alloy of copper, and tin, with trace elements derived from these and various other minerals, and a variable quantity of lead. In southern Britain lead commonly forms at least 1% of the alloy and usually about 3%, from the Wilburton phase (Brown and Blin-Stoyle, 1959), but in North Britain a significant proportion of lead is not usual until the Heathery Burn phase, while in Wales lead-bronze was used from the Acton Park phase (Northover, unpublished research). The purpose of the lead may have been to facilitate working at lower temperatures since the new alloy would be softer, or to economize slightly on the amount of copper used (Brown and Blin-Stoyle, 1959, 193). Also the metal would fill shrinkage cavities more readily, since the lead made the bronze more fluid (Tylecote, 1962, 44). In the Late Bronze Age, the founder relied heavily on the re-use of broken implements, as well as newly smelted bronze in the form of cake. This is demonstrated by the vast quantities of scrap metal occurring in some founder's hoards at this period. The bronze smith would have heated the required amount of bronze in a clay crucible to about $1000^{\circ}C$, so that it was well melted, and then poured the metal into a prepared mould, placed in a suitable position for casting, such as the pit of sand found beside sword and axe moulds and a hearth at Jarlshof (Curle, 1932-3, 92).

When the spearhead had been cast, allowed to cool, and the mould removed, it would have been finished off. The lozenge-shaped loops which occur on some spearheads would have been hammered down, since the cavities for the loops in the moulds are invariably semi-circular. In most cases, the casting flashes were removed. The bevelled edges, found on some spearheads, would for the most part have been the intentional result of the shape of the mould; however, where the bevelling is confined to a narrow area at the edge of the blade, it was probably due to hammering and sharpening of the edges. Little post-casting work of heat treatment seems to have been carried out, and is usually limited to local annealing of the metal during the process of hammering the edges in order to sharpen and harden them (Allen, Britton and Coghlan, 1970, 23).

The pegholes on pegged spearheads were made as part of the casting process, but those found on a few looped spearheads were probably later additions; this is particularly clear on Sparsholt (104), where the peghole is between the broken ends of the loop, and must have been drilled.

The incised decoration on some spearheads was probably chased, that is, a pointed tool held in one hand was driven along the surface of the bronze with a hammer (Lowery, Savage, and Wilkins, 1972, 172). Pointillé decoration, as seen on Taplow (121), and the notched decoration around the mouth of spearheads such as Burghfield (29), would also have been made by hammering a pointed or V-shaped tool held against the spearhead.

Hafting

Some bronze spearheads still have part of their shaft in the socket, and examination of shaft remains from elsewhere in the British Isles (Greenwell and Brewis, 1909, 467) has shown that they were usually made of ash, or sometimes pinewood. A pegged spearhead from Pokesdown, Hants. (Clay, 1927, 470) was found with the cast of its shaft, which was 7 feet long and broken. The diameter of the cast was just under 2 inches and the excavator considered that, allowing for some falling in of the walls of the cast after the wood had decayed, the diameter of the shaft would be well under two inches. A number of shaft fragments e.g. Wallingford (133) clearly show that they were carved to make the end conical, to produce a tight fit in the socket.

Looped spearheads were probably secured to their shafts with a cord, or leather thong, which passed through the loops of the spearhead, and through a hole in the shaft below the head, around a groove in the shaft, or around a peg glued into a hole in the shaft. In the case of pegged spearheads, a hole would have been drilled into the shaft opposite the pegholes. This can be seen in Wallingford (134), which still has the wooden peg in the hole. Two spearheads from the area, Windsor (145) and Sonning (102) have bronze pegs in situ in their shafts. Greenwell and Brewis (1909, 468) gave only three other examples of bronze pegs in this type of spearhead, one from the Lower Thames, one from Lakenheath, Suffolk, and one from Ireland, and suggested that wooden pegs were more usual. No chronological significance seems to be apparent in the two types, except that Sonning (102) with a bronze peg may be late; nor is it clear which is technically superior, for, while a wooden peg might break at both ends, flush with the shaft, a bronze one might be more likely to slip out of the wooden shaft.

The method of hafting a barbed spearhead has often been discussed. A simple shaft, held in place by the pegs, could not have been very secure, since the socket only extends a few centimetres. Bartlett and Hawkes (1965, 372) suggest that these may have been harpoons and had a wooden butt-piece, pegged into the socket, but emerging only as a short tongue. The top of the shaft was held in a split in the butt-piece by a thong. At the shock of impact this would come apart, leaving the spearhead sticking in the target, while the shaft fell loosely, still attached by the thong. A butt-piece would, however, be unnecessary. As has been pointed out above, the cross-section of the peg, where it survives, is rectangular, in the centre, but of circular cross-section at either end. This could serve no useful function for holding the shaft or butt-piece in place since a circular hole would have to be drilled into the wood, to fit the peg. But it could be used to support a split-ended shaft which was tied loosely to the ends of the pegs with a thong, and used as a harpoon (Atkinson, 1976, pers. comm.).

In the Late Bronze Age a butt or ferrule was sometimes fitted to the base of the shaft of spears, but it cannot have been universal practice in view of the vastly disproportionate number of heads and butts that have been found.

Use

There may have been a number of uses for spearheads in the Bronze Age. Some earlier writers distinguished between javelin points, lance heads and spearheads. The main difference is in the method of projection. The smaller spearheads have been called javelin points, implying that they were thrown, like a dart, while the larger ones, the lance heads, may have been used as thrusting weapons. Hodges (1957, 58) suggests that the lance-heads may have been used in war, while the javelin heads were used for hunting. He points out that the larger spearheads are more often found with swords, while the smaller ones occur in tool hoards. The presence of two forms of spearhead, side- and basal-looped, of different size in the Middle Bronze Age, is perhaps also an indication that the two types had different functions. The contrasting distribution of these two classes of spearhead in Berkshire, Buckinghamshire and Oxfordshire, (see p. 17 above) with the side-looped spearheads showing a widespread distribution typical of tool types, whereas the riverine distribution of basal-looped spearheads is typical of pegged spearheads and swords, may also suggest different uses for the different types.

Among the Iron Age rock carvings in the Camonica valley in N. Italy (Anati, 1964, 205) there is an illustration of a man apparently using a spear with an overarm thrusting action, piercing the body of another man, also carrying a spear, and there are other illustrations of spears being used in the same way for hunting animals. The basal-looped spearhead tip from Dorchester (54) found piercing a human pelvis, demonstrates their use in warfare, as do the two broken, leaf-shaped looped spearheads from Tormarton,

Glos. (Knight, Browne and Grinsell, 1972, 14), which were lodged in the spinal vertebrae and pelvis of a skeleton, which also had a wound in its skull. Beside it lay another victim with a spear wound in his pelvis. Another human skeleton from La Grotte du Pas de Joulie, Treves, in France, also had a bronze spearhead embedded in his vertebrae (Knight, Browne and Grinsell, 1972, 16).

It has frequently been suggested that some of the larger spearheads may have been used only for ceremonial purposes. The size of some spearheads, including many of the triangular bladed basal-looped spearheads would have made them rather unwieldy, and their decoration, as in the case of Taplow (121) which has gold studs, might make them too valuable to risk losing or damaging them. Also, the small diameter of the socket in proportion to their size may have made some of them unsatisfactory either for thrusting or throwing (Coles, Coutts and Ryder, 1964, 191). The large number of basal-looped spearheads, in contrast to the small number of side-looped spearheads, which were found in "watery" environments may also have some bearing on the use of the type as a ritual object.

Barbed spearheads may also have had a ceremonial or ritual function. The size of their blades and the proximity of the pins to the barbs would have caused them to be inefficient in preventing dislodgement. Evans (1881, 338) was the first to point out that they are too big to have been used as fish-spears, commenting that "they would have made sad havoc, even of a forty-pound salmon." Wild animal hunting seems to be ruled out by their distribution; almost all come from rivers (Burgess, Coombs and Davies, 1972, 226). But there are larger fish than forty-pound salmon. Sturgeon, which commonly grow to 700 lb and eight to twelve feet in length, and seasonally inhabit rivers and estuaries, might perhaps be considered as suitable candidates, particularly if the spearhead were hafted as a harpoon. (Atkinson, 1976, personal communication.) They have been caught in the past few centuries in many rivers in Britain, including the Thames, and twelfth century accounts speak of the ease with which sturgeon could be obtained at hostelries in the city of London (Fitzstephen, 1183); in the prehistoric period they were probably far more common in our rivers than today, since large-scale fishing over the past few centuries has almost certainly caused many species to become rarer, and to decline in size. Furthermore, in Russia, in the nineteenth century it was the practice to catch sturgeon with harpoons, when the fish had concentrated quietly near the river bank (Day, 1880-4, 282). While this suggestion cannot be proved, it may perhaps be considered as an alternative to their use as ceremonial objects (as suggested by Burgess, Coombs and Davies, 1972, 227 and other writers).

CHRONOLOGY AND CONCLUSIONS

An attempt has been made to fit the classes of spearheads into the accepted chronological phases and metal-working traditions of the Bronze Age. Little attention, however, has been given to the absolute chronology of these phases. This is particularly difficult, since there are as yet only a small number of fixed points, provided by radio-carbon dates, to work from, and the details of the correlation of British metalworking phases to European chronologies are arguable and based on a comparatively small number of links. An attempt to give absolute dates and the times at which each type of spearhead was in use is shown in Fig. 2 (the dates on this are based mainly on Burgess, 1976). However it is clearly important to remember that there would have been considerable overlap between spearhead types; for some time after a new type had been introduced, the older types would have remained the more popular, gradually giving way to the new types.

In conclusion, therefore, the large number of spearheads from Berkshire, Buckinghamshire and Oxfordshire testify both to the importance of the area during the Bronze Age, and to the importance of the spear as a weapon at that time - apparently much more so in the Bronze Age than in the preceding Neolithic or the succeeding Iron Age.

As has been shown, the spearheads are not evenly distributed over the area; over 50% were definitely found in the rivers Thames and Kennet, and another 20-30% were either found in the river or very close to the river banks; a large number of these were found below Marlow where the Thames is wider than most rivers in this country. This would seem to argue that the Thames held some great importance to Bronze Age man, either on religious grounds or its banks may have been a popular place for settlement.

The great variety of shapes and sizes of spearheads in the Bronze Age, which has been pointed out in earlier chapters, is a testimony of the artisan's skill in manufacture; the differences in the appearance of different types of spearhead is largely due to their method of attachment to the shaft, either by loops at the sides of the socket or at the base of the blade, or by pegs. These differences probably reflect an active exchange of ideas with other regions and the craftsman's creative inventiveness, so that very few spearheads are identical, and possibly also the different uses to which the various types of spearhead were put, some for warfare, others for hunting and perhaps others for ceremonial uses.

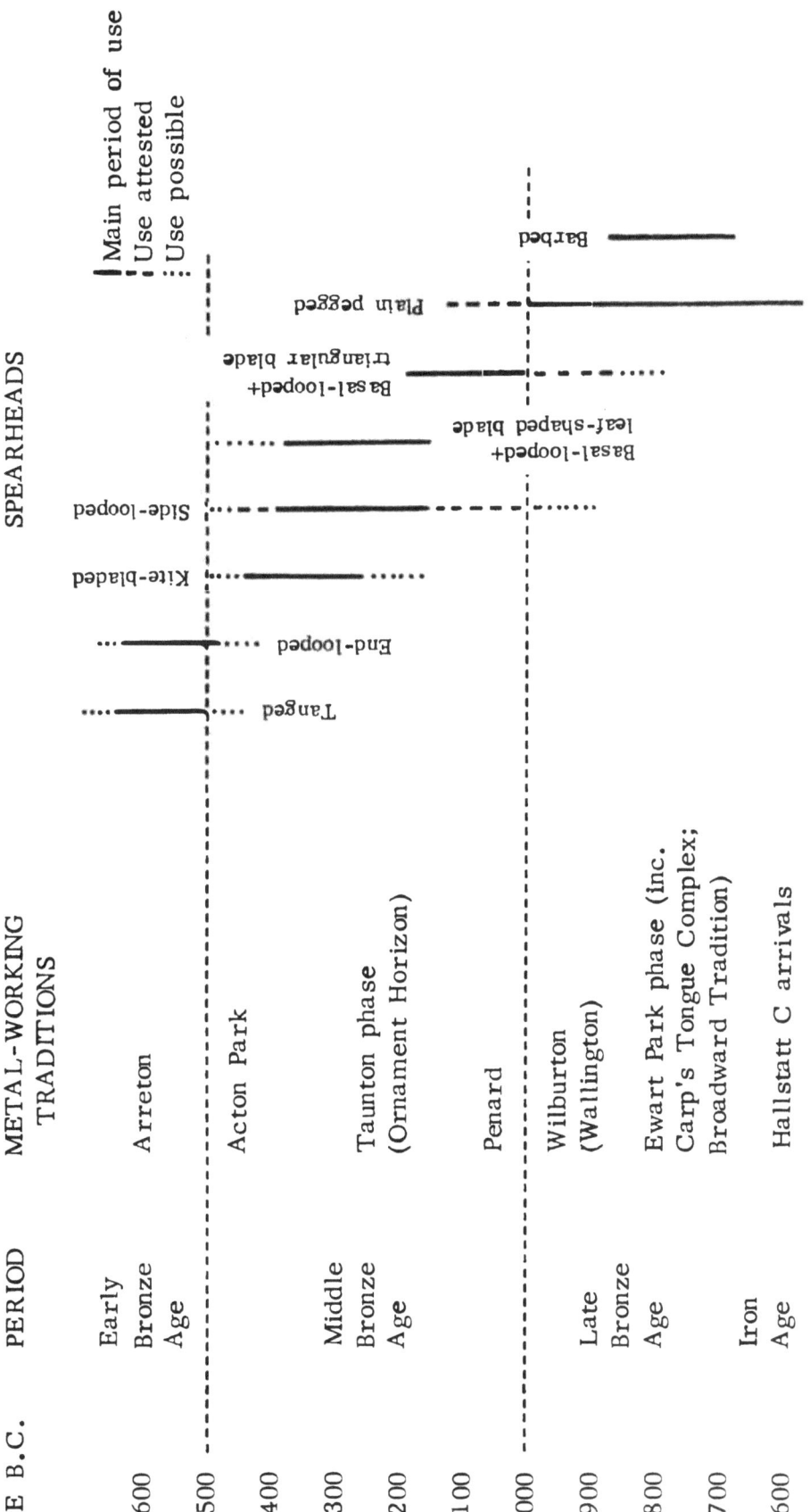

Fig. 2 Table Showing the Chronology of Spearhead Types.

CATALOGUE

Entries are set out as follows:-

No.	PROVENANCE	National Grid Reference	Present Location
	Details of Discovery		and Museum
	Bibliography		Assessions No.
	Description		
	Length x max. width (in mm)	Weight (in g)	
	Classification	Figure and Plate No.	

The provenance is given under parish and county, except in the case of hoards, where an accepted and well-used name, e.g. Burgesses' Meadow, is used in preference to the parish. The county boundary reorganization of April 1974 has affected a number of parishes within the area, although the outer limits of the area remain unchanged. Where this is so, the old county is given first to facilitate reference to previous work, the new county following in brackets.

The National Grid Reference is given to within as much accuracy as available information allows.

The description includes details of the present condition of the spearhead, the means of attachment to the shaft, the shape of the blade and midrib, and the socket. Any decoration is then described, followed by any evidence of the method of manufacture.

The classification is that of Greenwell and Brewis (1909). (See Fig. 1).

The following abbreviations are used in the Catalogue:-

a) <u>General</u>

    BICC   Bronze Implements Card Catalogue (housed in BM)
    c.   circa
    Fig.   figure
    g   grammes
    Info   information
    mm   millimetres
    OS cards   Ordnance Survey Record Cards
    Pl.   plate

b) <u>Present Location</u>

    Ash. M   Ashmolean Museum, Oxford (Dept. of Antiquities)

BM	British Museum, London (Dept. of Prehistoric and Romano-British Antiquities)
BuCM	Buckinghamshire County Museum, Aylesbury
CAE	University Museum of Archaeology and Ethnology, Cambridge
Canterbury	Royal Museum, Canterbury
Eton College	Myers Museum, Eton College, Eton
LM	London Museum, London
Newbury M	Borough Museum, Newbury
RM	Museum and Art Gallery, Reading
Windsor Guildhall	Guildhall Exhibition, Windsor
PLU	Present Location Unknown
(Benson Coll.)	J. W. Benson of Bond St., London no longer possesses any antiquities.
(Gieford Coll.)	Formerly owned by Dr. Hasting Gieford of Reading
(Hambledon)	The Museum, Hambledon, Bucks. closed in 1959 and all the contents are said to have been taken to Reading and Aylesbury Museums. However the relevant spearhead does not seem to be in either of these museums.
(Hatford)	formerly Hatford Manor
(Kinross Coll.)	This collection was formerly at Grove Ley, Feltham, but it is now lost. It may have found its way to America or Canada (Gowing, 1974, pers. comm. and OS cards).
(Lord Boston Coll.)	not in BuCM as OS cards suggest
(Martin Coll.)	M. C. Martin no longer lives in George Road, Egbaston as stated in BICC
(St. John Coll.)	Col. St. John no longer lives in Slinford, Essex
(Smith Coll.)	Although all the artefacts in the Smith Coll. are said to have been given to Reading Museum one spearhead (Sonning (103)) does not seem to have been included.
(Wells Coll.)	W. G. Wells no longer lives at 2 Maybank Ave., Wembley as stated in BICC

1.   ABINGDON, Berks (Oxon)   SU 4996   PLU

   'Found in or near Abingdon, dredged from Thames'
   Bibl: Smith, 1873, 430; Peake, 1931, 54
   Class V

2.   AKELEY, Bucks   SP 7137   CAE 48.315^A

   Bought at Stowe sale, 1849; ex-Braybrooke Coll.
   Lozenge-shaped side loops. Kite-shaped blade with lozenge-section midrib and ridge running along the top of it and continuing onto socket.
   146 mm x 32 mm
   Class III/IV   Fig. 3

3.   AKELEY, Bucks   SP 7137   CAE 48.315^B

   As above, but no indication whether or not these, with a bag-shaped axe, are a hoard.
   Leaf-shaped side loops near socket mouth. Dagger-shaped channelled blade. Socket does not extend into blade. Extensively decorated in bands of incised lines and pointillé dots above and below loops and at base of blade.
   130 mm x 39 mm
   Class II   Fig. 3

4.   AMERDEN, Bucks   SU 902805   BM 94.12-10.47

   From Thames (Not available for study. Info. from BICC)
   Lozenge-shaped side loops. Leaf-shaped blade with bevelled edges. Lozenge-section midrib.
   159 mm x 29 mm   75 g
   Class IV   Fig. 5

5.   AMERDEN, Bucks   SU 902805   BM 94.12-10.48

   From Thames
   Lozenge-shaped side loops. Leaf-shaped blade with circular-section midrib. Socket extends only slightly into blade. Casting flashes remain on sides of socket.
   124 mm x 22 mm   55 g
   Class IV   Fig. 4

6.   AMERDEN, Bucks   SU 902805   BM 94.12-10.49

   From Thames
   Ferrule. Tubular and slightly conical. Contains part of wooden shaft. Casting flashes remain on sides.
   220 mm x 25 mm   168 g
                                                               Fig. 26

7. AMERSHAM, Bucks   SU 963973   BuCM 15.57

From bed of river Misbourne
Tip bent. String side-loops. Ogival blade with lozenge-section midrib. Slight traces of casting flashes on sides of socket.
148 mm x 24 mm
Class IV   Fig. 10

8. AMERSHAM, Bucks   SU 9697   PLU

From Bury End (OS Cards)

9. ASHBURY, Berks (Oxon)   SU 281802   BM 55.10-18.7

From Botley Copse
Bibl: Evans, 1881, 322; Shrubsole, 1906, 194; Peake, 1931, 175
In two pieces. Lozenge-shaped side loops. Leaf-shaped blade with circular-section midrib.
109 mm x 19 mm   48 g
Class IV   Fig. 4

10. ASTON and COTE, Oxon.   SP 352033   Ash.M NC 406

Bibl: Manning and Leeds, 1921, 23; Leeds, 1939, 247
In two pieces. Lozenge-section side loops. Ogival blade with bevelled edges. Lozenge-section midrib. Mouth of socket indented. Casting flashes remain on sides of socket.
161 mm x 31 mm   68 g
Class IV   Fig. 10

11. AYLESBURY, Bucks   SP 817139   BuCM 246/08

Found among rubbish in donor's house, Church Street, Aylesbury. There is no evidence of original provenance. (Not marked on distribution maps.)
Tip and small part of blade missing. Leaf-shaped side loops. Leaf-shaped blade with bevelled edges and lozenge-section midrib. Traces of casting flashes on sides of socket.
119 mm x 23 mm
Class IV   Fig. 6

12. BENSON, Oxon   SU 613912   RM 12.62

From Thames at Benson Lock
Blade only. Elliptical blade with lozenge-section midrib.
153 mm x 38 mm   118 g
Class V?   Fig. 20

13. NEW BRADWELL, Bucks   SP 825413   Northampton Museum
                                                NN 1/12

Part of a hoard found in 1879, which was 'contained in a deep cist filled with black earth and about 1' 6" deep, and consisted of 16 pieces, namely 9 socketed celts, 3 broken celts, 1 palstave, 2 spearheads and

a leaf-shaped sword, broken into four pieces.
Bibl: Clinch 1905, 183; Kennett, 1969
Tip only of socketed spearhead
Class V

14. NEW BRADWELL, Bucks   SP 825413   Northampton Museum
NN 1/13
As above
Bibl: Clinch 1905, 183; Kennett, 1969
Tip only of a socketed spearhead
Class V

15. BRAY, Berks   SU 915795   RM 252:45/1

From Thames, 1909
Bibl: Smallcombe and Collins, 1946, 65; Burgess, Coombs and Davies, 1972, 244
Opposed pegholes, with a bronze peg, 56 mm long and rounded at both ends, in situ. Barbed, parallel-sided blade with ovate-section midrib. Part of wooden shaft remains in socket.
251 x 64 mm   260 g
Class VI   Fig. 24

16. BRAY, Berks   SU 915795   RM 252:45/2

From Thames, 1909
Bibl: Smallcombe and Collins, 1946, 65; Burgess, Coombs and Davies, 1972, 244
Opposed pegholes with a bronze peg, 54 mm long, rounded at both ends, in situ. Barbed, parallel-sided blade, with ovate-section midrib.
251 mm x 58 mm   290 g
Class VI   Fig. 24

17. BRAY, Berks   SU 910798   RM 110.51 (TCB 101)

From Thames above Bray Lock
Part of blade broken. Opposed pegholes. Elliptical blade, with bevelled edges and lozenge-section. No distinct midrib. Four circular openings on blade, the top two of which continue into spike-like openings.
451 x 70 mm   990 g
Class V   Fig. 23

18. BRAY, Berks   SU 915790   RM 42.53

From gravel pit, Monkey Island
Bibl: Burgess, Coombs and Davies, 1972, 244
Tip and socket mouth broken. Blade bent. Opposed pegholes. Barbed, parallel-sided blade with ovate-section midrib.
163 mm x 62 mm   190 g
Class VI   Fig. 25

19. BRAY, Berks   SU 915790   RM 43.53

From gravel pit, Monkey Island
Tip missing. Lozenge-shaped basal loops. Ogival channelled blade, with lozenge-section midrib.
157 mm x 43 mm   138 g
Class III A   Fig. 14

20. BRAY, Berks   SU 923778   RM 170.53 (TCB 122)

From Thames at Oakley Court
Part of blade broken. Lanceolate blade with four pairs of circular openings, the top pair of which continue upwards into a spike-shaped opening. Midrib and socket have hexagonal cross-section.
428 mm x 78 mm   420 g
Class V   Fig. 23

21. BRAY, Berks   SU 9179   RM 151:63

From Hoveringham Gravel Pit
Bent, and socket broken. Opposed pegholes. Ogival blade with bevelled edge. Circular-section midrib.
178 mm x 35 mm   139 g
Class V   Fig. 21

22. BRAY, Berks   SU 9079   RM 1044:64

Opposed pegholes. Ogival blade with bevel very near to edge of blade. Circular-section midrib. Decorated with three bands of 6 incised lines between mouth of socket and pegholes. Part of wooden shaft remains in socket.
120 mm x 26 mm   66 g
Class V   Fig. 21

23. BRAY, Berks   SU 9179   Private Collection
                                                    (Inaccessible)
From Hoveringham Gravel Pit
Bibl: Rutland and Greenaway, 1970, 55
Tip broken. Lozenge-shaped basal loops. 'Ridge down each face of blade'.
160 mm
Class III A

24. BURGESSES' MEADOW, Oxon   SP 502074   Ash.M NC 405

Found in a field near Oxford, 1830 with a flat tanged knife, unlooped palstave, chisel, socketed hammer of leaded bronze, rod-shaped ingot and another spearhead 25 below.
Bibl: Leeds, 1916, 147; Leeds, 1939, 247; Hawkes, 1954, G.B. 6; Manning and Leeds, 1921, 251; Smith, 1959a, 171; Brown and Blin-Stoyle, 1959, 201
Blade broken. String side loops. Leaf-shaped blade with circular-section midrib.

Non-leaded bronze (Brown and Blin-Stoyle, 1959, 201)
110 mm x 31 mm   74 g
Class IV   Fig. 8

25. BURGESSES' MEADOW, Oxon   SP 502074   Ash.M NC 404

    As 24 above
    Bibl: as 24 above.
    Edges of blade broken. String side loops. Also one peghole near socket mouth. Leaf-shaped blade with lozenge-section midrib.
    215 mm x 33 mm   104 g
    Class IV   Fig. 9

26. BURGHFIELD, Berks   SU 6470   RM 249:45

    From Kennet
    Bibl: Peake, 1931, 185; Smallcombe and Collins, 1946, 65
    String side loops near base of blade. Narrow leaf-shaped blade with lozenge-section midrib.
    174 mm x 19 mm   67 g
    Class IV   Fig. 9

27. BURGHFIELD, Berks   SU 6470   RM 250:45

    From Kennet
    Bibl: Peake, 1931, 185; Smallcombe and Collins, 1946, 65
    Tip slightly bent. Lozenge-shaped side loops. Leaf-shaped blade with bevelled edges. Circular-section midrib. Casting flashes remain on sides of socket.
    157 mm x 31 mm   68 g
    Class IV   Fig. 4

28. BURGHFIELD, Berks   SU 682704   RM 18:60

    From Messrs. Hyde Crete's gravel pit
    Bibl: BAJ, 1960, 55
    Part of blade broken. String side loops. Leaf-shaped blade with lozenge-section midrib. Small notches at 1 mm intervals around mouth of socket. Part of wooden shaft remains in socket.
    112 mm x 20 mm   34 g
    Class IV   Fig. 7

29. BURGHFIELD, Berks   SU 654708   RM 43:60

    Found beside R. Kennet in material which had apparently been spread from dredgings of the river.
    Bibl: BAJ, 1960, 55
    Bent and damaged in places. Opposed pegholes. Lanceolate blade with bevelled edges. Circular-section midrib.
    248 mm x 52 mm   250 g
    Class V   Fig. 19

30. CAVERSHAM, Berks   SU 725743   Canterbury 2078

   Dredged from Thames
   Bibl: Grove, 1953, 118
   Edges of blade damaged. In two pieces. Narrow basal loops.
   Triangular channelled blade, with circular-section midrib.
   367 mm x 45 mm
   Class III A   Fig. 16

31. EAST CHALLOW, Berks (Oxon) SU 3888   PLU (Wells Coll.)

   Bibl: Roskill, 1938, 19; Peake, 1931, 42
   Basal loops. Triangular channelled blade, circular-section midrib.
   247 mm x 48 mm   248.09 g
   Class III A   Fig. 17

32. CLEWER, Berks   SU 937772   RM 56.50 (TCB 86)

   From Thames at Surley Hall Point
   One loop broken. Lozenge-shaped basal loops. Leaf-shaped channelled blade with lozenge-section midrib. Part of wooden shaft remains in socket.
   259 mm x 49 mm
   Class III A   Fig. 14

33. CLEWER, Berks   SU 9677   PLU (Wells Coll.)

   From Thames
   Opposed pegholes. Lanceolate lozenge-section hollow blade. No distinction between wings and midrib.
   154 mm x 36 mm   99.22 g
   Class V   Fig. 20

34. COOKHAM, Berks   SU 868870   BM 1905.7-13.1

   Found by dredgers between Stone House and Spade Oak Ferry
   Bibl: Peake, 1931, 190; Butler, 1963, 108
   Opposed pegholes. Lanceolate blade with bevelled edges. Midrib circular-sectioned but finishes 50 mm from tip. Mouth of socket bevelled.
   192 mm x 58 mm   192 g
   Class V   Fig. 22

35. COOKHAM, Berks   SU 8985   RM 60.48 (AL 6)

   From Thames
   String side loops. Ogival blade with lozenge-section midrib.
   150 mm x 27 mm   55 g
   Class IV   Fig. 10

36. COOKHAM, Berks   SU 8985   RM 64.48/1 (AL 9)
   From Thames
   Opposed pegholes. Lanceolate blade with bevelled edges and circular-

section midrib. Casting flashes remain on one side of socket.
96 mm x 33 mm   65 g
Class V   Fig. 22

37. COOKHAM, Berks   SU 8985   RM 64.48/2(AL 10)

   Found in Thames with 36 (Cookham)
   Socket partly broken. Opposed pegholes. Elliptical blade with bevelled edges and circular-section midrib.
   141 mm x 32 mm   78 g
   Class V   Fig. 18

38. COOKHAM, Berks   SU 897856   RM 209.58 (TCB 179)

   From Cookham Weir
   Bibl: BAJ, 1959, 119
   Opposed pegholes. Elliptical blade with bevelled edges. Circular-section midrib.
   124 mm x 26 mm   84 g
   Class V   Fig. 18

39. COOKHAM, Berks   SU 897856   LM 42.14/3

   Dredged from Thames at Cookham Weir
   Bibl: Baynes, 1921, 316
   Narrow basal loops. Also two small opposed pegholes. Triangular channelled blade with circular-section midrib.
   470 mm x 54 mm   350 g
   Class III A   Fig. 16

40. CREMORNE ?   PLU

   From Thames
   Bibl: Smith, 1861, 161; Smith, 1873, 430.

41. CULHAM, Oxon   SU 504949   Ash.M 1927.2703

   Ex-Evans Collection
   Bibl: Evans, 1881, 320; Manning and Leeds, 1921, 239; Leeds, 1939, 249
   Opposed pegholes. Slightly ogival blade with circular-section midrib. Decorated with four bands of four incised lines around mouth of socket. Above are four incised dashed lines.
   87 mm x 23 mm   38 g
   Class V   Fig. 21

42. DATCHET, Bucks (Berks)   SU 9876   BM 56.7-1.1371

   From Thames, ex-Roach Smith Coll.
   Bibl: Evans, 1881, 330; Clinch, 1905, 183; Brown and Blin-Stoyle, 1959, 203
   One loop missing and blade damaged. Leaf-shaped basal loops. Triangular channelled blade with lozenge-section midrib. Part of shaft

remains in socket.
Non-leaded bronze (Brown and Blin-Stoyle, 1959, 203)
560 mm x 57 mm   371 g
Class III A   Fig. 14

43.   DATCHET, Bucks (Berks)   SU 9876   LM A17919

From Thames
Bibl: Peake, 1931, 245
String side loops. Leaf-shaped blade with lozenge-section midrib. Casting flashes remain on sides of socket.
138 mm x 26 mm
Class IV   Fig. 8

44.   DATCHET, Bucks (Berks)   SU 9876   Windsor Guildhall R149

Opposed pegholes. Lanceolate blade with slightly bevelled edges and lozenge-section midrib.
211 mm x 41 mm
Class V   Fig. 20

45.   DATCHET, Bucks (Berks)   SU 9876   PLU (Kinross Coll.)

From Thames
Tanged blade, with rivet-hole at end of tang. Triangular blade with shallow midrib outlined by three incised lines.
175 mm x 34 mm
Class I   Fig. 3

46.   DATCHET, Bucks (Berks)   SU 9876   PLU (Kinross Coll.)

From Thames
Basal loops. Triangular blade
199 mm x 37 mm
Class III A   Fig. 17

47.   DATCHET, Bucks (Berks)   SU 9876   PLU (Kinross Coll.)

From Thames
Part of socket broken. Basal loops. Triangular channelled blade.
246 mm x 45 mm
Class III A   Fig. 15

48.   DATCHET, Bucks (Berks)   SU 9876   PLU (Kinross Coll.)

From Thames
Side loops. Leaf-shaped blade with lozenge-section midrib.
106 mm x 23 mm
Class IV   Fig. 7

49. DATCHET, Bucks (Berks)　　SU 9876　　　　PLU (Kinross Coll.)

   From Thames
   Opposed pegholes. Ogival blade with circular-section midrib.
   116 mm x 31 mm
   Class V　　　　　　　　　　　　　　　Fig. 21

50. DATCHET, Bucks (Berks)　　SU 9876　　　　PLU (Kinross Coll.)

   From Thames
   Opposed pegholes. Ogival blade with circular-section midrib.
   156 mm x 35 mm
   Class V　　　　　　　　　　　　　　　Fig. 21

51. DATCHET, Bucks (Berks)　　SU 9876　　　　PLU (Kinross Coll.)

   From Thames
   Opposed pegholes? Lanceolate blade with circular-section midrib.
   247 mm x 41 mm
   Class V　　　　　　　　　　　　　　　Fig. 22

52. DATCHET, Bucks (Berks)　　SU 9876　　　　PLU (Kinross Coll.)

   From Thames
   Opposed pegholes? Lanceolate blade with circular-section midrib.
   184 mm x 51 mm
   Class V　　　　　　　　　　　　　　　Fig. 19

53. DATCHET, Bucks (Berks)　　SU 9876　　　　PLU (Kinross Coll.)

   From Thames
   Opposed pegholes. Lanceolate blade with circular-section midrib.
   121 mm x 27 mm
   Class V　　　　　　　　　　　　　　　Fig. 22

54. DORCHESTER, Oxon　　　　SU 583949　　　Ash.M Loan from
   　　　　　　　　　　　　　　　　　　　　　　　R. Hatt
   Found impaling the pelvis of a human skeleton, with a skull and thin
   perforated stone at Queensford Mill.
   Bibl: Hewett, 1902, 31; Leeds, 1939, 263
   Tip only. Channelled blade with circular-section midrib.
   117 mm x 27 mm　　　　　　　　　36 g
   Class III A　　　　　　　　　　　　　Fig. 15 Pl. 1

55. ETON, Bucks (Berks)　　　SU 970778　　　Eton College 196

   Dredged from Thames
   Tip bent. Leaf-shaped basal loops. Leaf-shaped channelled blade
   with lozenge-section midrib.
   225 mm x 52 mm　　　　　　　　　220 g
   Class III A　　　　　　　　　　　　　Fig. 13

56. ETON, Bucks (Berks)   SU 970778   Eton College 191
   Dredged from Thames
   Lozenge-shaped side loops. Leaf-shaped blade with oval-section midrib.
   142 mm x 26 mm   67 g
   Class IV   Fig. 4

57. ETON, Bucks (Berks)   SU 970778   Eton College 194
   Dredged from Thames
   Lozenge-section side loops. Leaf-shaped blade with bevelled edges. Lozenge-section midrib. Casting flashes remain on sides of socket.
   157 mm x 30 mm   72 g
   Class IV   Fig. 5

58. ETON, Bucks (Berks)   SU 970778   Eton College 193
   Dredged from Thames
   String side loops. Ogival blade with bevelled edges and lozenge-section midrib. Part of wooden shaft remains in socket. Casting flashes remain on sides of socket.
   136 mm x 25 mm   55 g
   Class IV   Fig. 10

59. ETON, Bucks (Berks)   SU 970778   PLU (formerly at Eton College)
   Dredged from Thames
   Tip of blade broken. Side loops. Leaf-shaped blade.
   100 mm x 29 mm   44 g
   Class IV   Fig. 6

60. ETON, Bucks (Berks)   SU 970778   Eton College 192
   Dredged from Thames
   Opposed pegholes. Lanceolate blade with circular-section midrib.
   171 mm x 32 mm   110 g
   Class V   Fig. 19

61. FYFIELD, Berks (Oxon)   SU 4298   Ash.M 1927.2706
   ex-Evans Collection
   Bibl: Evans, 1881, 322; Shrubsole, 1906, 182; Peake, 1931, 197; Brown and Blin-Stoyle, 1959, 202
   Lozenge-section side loops. Leaf-shaped blade with lozenge-section midrib. Mouth of socket bevelled. Leaded Bronze. (Brown and Blin-Stoyle, 1959, 202)
   156 mm x 25 mm   98 g
   Class IV   Fig. 6

62. HAGBOURNE HILL, Berks (Oxon)   SU 497870   BM 61.9-20.6

   Part of a hoard found beside the Icknield Way and containing bronze collars, discs, a socketed axe and one or two other spearheads, probably from the same mould, as well as La Tène objects. See Appendix II
   Bibl: King, 1812, 348; Evans, 1881, 322; Evans, A., 1908, 31; Peake, 1931, 199
   String side loops. Leaf-shaped blade with lozenge-section midrib. Casting flashes remain on sides of socket.
   97 mm x 18 mm   29 g
   Class IV   Fig. 8

63. HAGBOURNE HILL, Berks (Oxon)   SU 490870   BM 62.7-19.10

   Part of hoard, see 62 above, and Appendix II
   Bibl: as 62 above
   Tip of blade missing. String side loops. Leaf-shaped blade with lozenge-section midrib. Casting flashes remain on side of socket.
   71 mm x 16 mm   24 g
   Class IV   Fig. 8

64. HAGBOURNE HILL, Berks (Oxon)   SU 490870   BM 62.7-19.11

   Possibly also from Hagbourne Hill hoard, see 62 above and Appendix II
   Bibl: as 62 above
   Tip only. Lozenge-section midrib.
   61 mm x 25 mm
   Class IV ?   Fig. 11

65. HATFORD, Berks (Oxon)   SU 326953   PLU (Hatford)

   Found buried 6 ft deep in peat near Hatford Brook, 1936
   Bibl: Underhill, 1938, 24
   String side loops broken. Leaf-shaped blade with lozenge-section midrib.
   190 mm x 30 mm   47 g
   Class IV   Fig. 9

66. HEADINGTON, Oxon   SP 566079   Ash.M 1921.79

   Found on surface by the old quarry, 240 yds NE of Shotover Lodge, Sandhills, 1892
   Bibl: Manning, 1898, 18; Manning and Leeds, 1921, 245; Leeds, 1939, 249
   Opposed pegholes. Ogival blade with circular-section midrib and slightly bevelled edges.
   125 mm x 33 mm   85 g
   Class V   Fig. 21

67.   HEDSOR, Bucks   SU 911860   PLU (Lord Boston Coll.)
      Dredged from Thames
      Basal loops. Leaf-shaped channelled blade with circular-section midrib.
      125 mm x 27 mm   58 g
      Class III A   Fig. 17

68.   NORTH HINKSEY, Berks   SP 498053   Ash.M 1921.82
      Dredged up at south end of Minster Ditch, 1895. One of four bronzes, including 69 below, a socketed axe and a chisel dredged up in the 1890s. There is no further evidence to indicate whether or not these constitute a hoard.
      Bibl: Manning and Leeds, 1921, 263; Peake, 1931, 202
      Tip only. Lozenge-section midrib.
      96 mm x 30 mm   23 g
      Class IV ?   Fig. 11

69.   NORTH KINKSEY, Berks   SP 498053   Ash.M 1921.84
      Dredged from Minster Ditch c. 1897
      Bibl: Manning and Leeds, 1921, 251; Leeds, 1939, 247; Brown and Blin-Stoyle, 1959, 201
      String side loops. Leaf-shaped blade with lozenge-section midrib.
      Non-leaded bronze (Brown and Blin-Stoyle, 1959, 247)
      96 mm x 23 mm   26 g
      Class IV   Fig. 8

70.   IVINGHOE BEACON, Bucks   SP 960169   BuCM
      From excavation of hillfort, 1963-5 (Site Ax)
      Bibl: Britton, 1968b, 207
      Fragment, "perhaps from the blade of a spearhead"
      24 mm x 7 mm

71.   KINTBURY, Berks   SU 339693   Newbury M OA 262
      Found near Eddington Mill, just north of Kennet, 1927
      Bibl: Roskill, 1938, 19; Coghlan, 1966, 185
      Tip broken. Leaf-shaped side loops. Ogival blade with lozenge-section midrib.
      210 mm x 33 mm   112 g
      Class IV   Fig. 10

72.   LITTLEMORE, Oxon   SP 5402   PLU
      Bibl: Smith, 1854, 186; Smith, 1873, 430; Manning and Leeds, 1921
      Side loops. 'Point slightly bulbous'
      Class IV

73. MAIDENHEAD, Berks   SU 9082   BM WG 1647

   From Thames
   Socket and blade bent. Opposed pegholes. Lanceolate blade with circular-section midrib.
   127 mm x 33 mm   77 g
   Class V   Fig. 22

74. MAIDENHEAD, Berks   SU 9082   BM WG 1648

   Found with 72 above, in Thames
   Opposed pegholes. Lanceolate blade with slightly bevelled edges and circular-section midrib. Casting flashes remain on one side of socket.
   92 mm x 32 mm   70 g
   Class V   Fig. 22

75. MAIDENHEAD, Berks   SU 9082   BM 1960.11-17.6

   From Thames. Probably ex-Knowles Coll.
   Part of blade only. Blade probably leaf-shaped with slightly bevelled edges and lozenge-section midrib.
   93 mm x 41 mm
   Class V ?   Fig. 18

76. MAIDENHEAD, Berks   SU 9082   Ash.M 1887.2549

   From Thames
   Bibl: Peake, 1931, 211
   Opposed pegholes. Lanceolate blade with bevelled edges and circular-section midrib. Decoration consists of 5 bands of four incised lines around mouth of socket, extending 14 mm from base, above which is a band of 3 incised dashed lines.
   150 mm x 31 mm   112 g
   Class V   Fig. 21

77. MAIDENHEAD, Berks   SU 902805   RM 68.52 (TCB 112)

   From Thames, downstream from railway bridge
   Bibl: Burgess, Coombs and Davies, 1972, 244
   Base of socket broken. Opposed pegholes with bronze peg, 62 mm long, rounded at both ends. Blade parallel-sided with barbs and ovate-section midrib. Part of wooden shaft remains in socket.
   269 mm x 65 mm   340 g
   Class VI   Fig. 24

78. MAIDENHEAD, Berks   SU 902805   RM 99.52 (TCB 116)

   From Thames, downstream from railway bridge
   Base of socket broken. Narrow basal loops. Triangular channelled blade, with circular-section midrib.
   291 mm x 45 mm   190 g
   Class III A   Fig. 17

79. MARLOW, Bucks   SU 8586   BuCM 110.55

Dredged from Thames
Lozenge-shaped basal loops; Leaf-shaped channelled blade with lozenge-section midrib, with narrow ridge running along top of each face.
226 mm x 43 mm
Class III A   Fig. 13

80. MEDMENHAM, Bucks   SU 818844   PLU (Hambledon)

From Danesfield, near Dane's Dyke
Side loops. Leaf-shaped blade
128 mm x 33 mm   92 g
Class IV   Fig. 7

81. MOLLINGTON, Oxon   SP 4247   County Museum, Warwick

From Lower Farm, Mollington with 82-84 and a chape. This is one of Burgess, Coombs and Davies (1972) Series I spearhead hoards.
Bibl: Burgess, Coombs and Davies, 1972, 239
Opposed pegholes. Lanceolate blade with bevelled edges and circular-section midrib.
224 mm x 34 mm
Class V

82. MOLLINGTON, Oxon   SP 4247   County Museum, Warwick

As 81 above
Bibl: as 81 above
Opposed pegholes. Lanceolate blade with bevelled edges and circular-section midrib.
192 mm x 52 mm
Class V

83. MOLLINGTON, Oxon   SP 4247   County Museum, Warwick

As 81 above
Bibl: as 81 above
Opposed pegholes. Lanceolate semi-hollow blade with bevelled edges and circular-section midrib.
190 mm x 42 mm
Class V

84. MOLLINGTON, Oxon   SP 4247   County Museum, Warwick

As 81 above
Bibl: as 81 above
Opposed pegholes. Lanceolate stepped and hollow blade.
160 mm x 37 mm
Class V

85.   MOULSFORD, Berks   SU 592838   RM 63.48 AL 11

From Thames
Bibl: Shrubsole, 1906, 181; Manning and Leeds, 1921, 263; Peake, 1931, 212; Leeds, 1939, 249; Roskill, 1938, 25; Burgess, Coombs and Davies, 1972, 244
Opposed pegholes. Leaf-shaped blade with small barbs and bevelled edges. Blade lozenge-sectioned, no distinct midrib.
321 mm x 64 mm   450 g
Class VI   Fig. 25

86.   NEWBURY, Berks   SU 458666   BM WG 2073

Found when making railway cutting
Bibl: Palmer, 1860, 322; Palmer, 1873, 429; Shrubsole, 1906, 181; Greenwell and Brewis, 1909, 47; Peake, 1931, 56; Roskill, 1938, 14
Tanged, with rivethole at base of tang. Triangular blade with ovate midrib outlined by slight step, and with bevelled edges.
181 mm x 37 mm   91 g
Class I   Fig. 3

87.   ?NEWBURY, Berks   SU 458666   PLU

?Found when making railway cutting, with 85 above; not mentioned in the earlier sources, and may never have existed.
Bibl: Roskill, 1938, 14
Said (Roskill, 1938, 14) to be identical to 85
Class I

88.   NEWBURY, Berks   SU 473673   Newbury M. OA 260

Found in peaty soil in Victoria Park, Newbury, 1933
Bibl: Coghlan, 1966, 187
Socket broken. Part of one loop just visible above break. Leaf-shaped blade with bevelled edges and circular-section midrib. Casting flashes remain on sides of socket.
110 mm x 29 mm   37 g
Class IV

89.   NEWBURY, Berks   SU 4564   Newbury M. 1939.69

From Watercress Beds
Bibl: Underhill, 1946, 55
Edges of blade and both loops broken off. Leaf-shaped blade with circular-section midrib. Part of wooden shaft remains in socket.
99 mm x 21 mm   66 g
Class IV   Fig. 4

90.   PADWORTH, Berks   SU 606669   PLU (formerly RM 121.57)

In a gravel pit near Padworth Mill
Bibl: Wymer, 1958, 58

String loops. Leaf-shaped blade.
94 mm x 19 mm   32 g
Class IV   Fig. 7

91. PRINCES RISBOROUGH, Bucks SP 804036   BuCM 145.12

From the Mount
Blade bent. String side loops. Leaf-shaped blade with lozenge-section midrib.
102 mm x 15 mm
Class IV   Fig. 7

92. PRINCES RISBOROUGH, Bucks SP 820042   BuCM 190.72

Found near Whiteleaf
Bibl: Farley, 1972, 215
Lozenge-shaped side loops. Leaf-shaped blade with lozenge-section midrib.
121 mm x 33 mm   76 g
Class IV   Fig. 7

93. PUSEY, Berks (Oxon)   SU 358979   Ash. M 1927.2705

ex-Evans Collection
Bibl: Brown and Blin-Stoyle, 1959, 202
Tip of blade broken. Lozenge-shaped side loops, outlined by a row of pointillé decoration. Leaf-shaped blade with bevelled edges. Lozenge-section midrib outlined by a row of pointillé decoration. Mouth of socket bevelled and also outlined in pointillé. Part of wooden shaft remains in socket.
175 mm x 35 mm   106 g
Class IV   Fig. 5

94. PUSEY, Berks (Oxon)   SU 358979   Ash. M 1927.2704

Found 1882. There is no evidence to suggest whether or not this and 93 constitute a hoard.
Opposed pegholes. Lanceolate blade with bevelled edges and circular-section midrib.
87 mm x 31 mm   52 g
Class V   Fig. 22

95. READING, Berks   SU 7173   PLU (Formerly RM 17.39)

Found in Reading
Bibl: Underhill, 1946, 56

96. READING, Berks   SU 7173   PLU (Gieford Coll.)

Found opposite house called Wyngates, Grosvenor Road, (now Cressington Road) in road making 1907
Bibl: BAJ, XXIV, 124
Part of blade only. Lanceolate, stepped and hollow blade.
133 mm x 44 mm
Class V   Fig. 20

97. READING, Berks   SU 7173   PLU (Martin Coll.)

Bibl: Peake, 1931, 57
Opposed pegholes. Lanceolate blade with bevelled edges and circular-section midrib.
163 mm x 37 mm
Class V   Fig. 18

98. READING, Berks   SU 7173   PLU (Wells Coll.)

From Kennet
Side loops. Kite-shaped blade with bevelled edge. Lozenge-section midrib. V-shaped rib on blade parallel to edge.
144 mm x 34 mm   78 g
Class III   Fig. 3

99. SANDFORD, Oxon   SP 531013   Ash.M 1885.509

Dredged from lock c. 1845
Bibl: Evans, 1881, 249; Manning and Leeds, 1921, 264; Peake, 1931, 52
Leaf-shaped basal loops, and opposed pegholes. Leaf-shaped blade with bevelled edge and lozenge-section midrib. Traces of casting flashes remain on one side of socket.
253 mm x 58 mm   330 g
Class III A   Fig. 14

100. SAUNDERTON, Bucks   SP 798022   BuCM 85.56

Found in 1954 in a patch of land on left side of road from railway bridge to Saunderton, just before bungalow named 'Purbeck'. Blade Blade only. Probably side looped. Leaf-shaped blade with circular-section midrib.
62 mm x 19 mm
Class IV ?   Fig. 11

101. SHIFFORD, Oxon   SU 357996   RM 269.47 (TCB 75)

From Thames at Tenfoot Bridge
Leaf-shaped side loops. Leaf-shaped blade with bevelled edges and lozenge-section midrib. V-shaped notches around mouth of socket and five short incised grooves between base of blade and loops on each side.
128 mm x 24 mm   55 g
Class IV   Fig. 6

102. SONNING, Berks   SU 757760   RM 72.55

From Thames
Opposed pegholes near mouth of socket. Small narrow elliptical blade with lozenge section. Three moulded bands around mouth of socket.
164 mm x 30 mm   116 g
Class V - Hallstatt ?   Fig. 22

103.   SONNING, Berks   SU 7576   PLU (Smith Coll.)

Side loops. Leaf-shaped blade with circular-section midrib.
132 mm x 23 mm   35 g
Class IV   Fig. 4

104.   SPARSHOLT, Berks (Oxon)   SU 345886   Ash.M NC 407

Probably from a canal near Sparsholt
Bibl: Peake, 1931, 227; Roskill, 1938, 17; Brown and Blin-Stoyle, 1959, 201.
Leaf-shaped side loops, one of which has been broken off, and a peg-hole drilled between the remaining stubs of the loops. Wide leaf-shaped blade with bevelled edges and circular-section midrib. Extensive decoration on socket and blade, comprising bands of incised lines and hatched triangles and dotted lines.
Non-leaded bronze (Brown and Blin-Stoyle, 1959, 201)
133 mm x 49 mm   137 g
Class III/IV   Fig. 7

105.   SPEEN, Berks   SU 412698   Newbury M. OA 263

From Hoe Benham
Bibl: Coghlan, 1966, 186
String side loops. Leaf-shaped blade with lozenge-section midrib and bevelled edges. Casting flashes remain on sides of socket.
103 mm x 16 mm
Class IV

106.   SPEEN, Berks   SU 4567   PLU (St. John Coll.)

Found in peat on Speen Moor in Kennet Valley, with 107 below. The find is typical of Burgess, Coombs and Davies (1972) series I spearhead hoards, which occur over a wide area of central southern England during the later part of the Bronze Age.
Bibl: Bunny, 1860, 322; Franks, 1865, 166; Evans, 1881, 337; Evans, 1873, 404; Shrubsole, 1906, 180; Peake, 1922, 128; Roskill, 1938, 19; Burgess, Coombs and Davies, 1972, 236
Basal loops. Leaf-shaped channelled blade with lozenge-section midrib.
176 mm x 37 mm   170 g
Class III A   Fig. 14

107.   SPEEN, Berks   SU 4567   PLU (St. John Coll.)

Found with 106 above
Bibl: as 106 above
Opposed pegholes near base of blade. Barbed, parallel-sided blade with ovate-section midrib defined by a slight step.
251 mm x 71 mm   397 g
Class VI   Fig. 25

108. STANDLAKE, Oxon   SP 397045   Ash.M 1911.137

   Found in Clark's Meadow
   Bibl: Manning and Leeds, 1921, 256; Leeds, 1939, 247
   Tip bent. String side loops near to base of blade. Leaf-shaped
   blade with lozenge-section midrib.
   139 mm x 28 mm   60 g
   Class IV   Fig. 9

109. STRATFIELD MORTIMER, Berks   SU 6563   RM 61.48 (AL 7)

   Found in a field at Mortimer West End, 1883
   Bibl: Shrubsole, 1906, 195; Peake, 1931, 230
   Narrow basal loops. Triangular channelled blade with circular-
   section midrib.
   212 mm x 36 mm   200 g
   Class III A   Fig. 17

110. TAPLOW, Bucks   SU 907845   BM 98.2-20.1

   Found in Thames
   Opposed pegholes near base of blade. Also another hole, nearer socket
   mouth, not in plane of wings, with rivet head in place. Lanceolate
   stepped blade. Circular-section midrib. Incised decoration in 4 bands
   of 3 parallel rows around socket, and pointillé defining step and midrib
   on blade.
   228 mm x 41 mm   187 g
   Class V   Fig. 21

111. TAPLOW, Bucks   SU 907845   BM 98.2-20.2

   Found in Thames
   Socket mouth damaged. Opposed pegholes and another hole nearer
   socket mouth. Elliptical blade with circular-section midrib.
   154 mm x 31 mm   109 g
   Class V   Fig. 18

112. TAPLOW, Bucks   SU 907845   BM 98.2-20.3

   Found in Thames
   Socket mouth slightly broken. Opposed pegholes. Elliptical blade
   with bevelled edges. Circular-section midrib.
   187 mm x 35 mm   112 g
   Class V   Fig. 20

113. TAPLOW, Bucks   SU 9081   BM 98.7-12.12

   From a creek near Taplow
   Bibl: Clinch, 1905, 18; Shrubsole, 1906, 185
   Opposed pegholes. Elliptical blade with circular-section midrib.
   165 mm x 33 mm   127 g
   Class V   Fig. 18

114.   TAPLOW, Bucks   SU 9081   BM 98.7-12.13

   From a creek near Taplow
   Bibl: as 113 above
   Tip bent, hole in socket. Opposed pegholes. Lanceolate blade with circular-section midrib. Part of wooden shaft remains in socket.
   211 mm x 43 mm   154 g
   Class V   Fig. 19

115.   TAPLOW, Bucks   SU 9081   BM 98.7-12.14

   From a creek near Taplow
   Bibl: as 113 above
   Opposed pegholes near base of blade. Lanceolate blade with bevelled edges and circular-section midrib.
   178 mm x 42 mm   150 g
   Class V   Fig. 20

116.   TAPLOW, Bucks   SU 9081   BM 98.7-12.15

   From a creek near Taplow
   Bibl: as Taplow 113 above
   Opposed pegholes. Narrow lanceolate blade with bevelled edges. Circular-section midrib, with little distinction between it and wings.
   198 mm x 32 mm   153 g
   Class V   Fig. 20

117.   TAPLOW, Bucks   SU 9081   BM 98.7-12.16

   Found in a creek near Taplow
   Bibl: as Taplow 113 above
   Tip bent and broken and blade damaged. Opposed pegholes. Lanceolate stepped blade with bevelled edges. Circular-section midrib. Decoration of parallel engraved lines in a band at mouth of socket.
   194 mm x 32 mm   158 g
   Class V   Fig. 20

118.   TAPLOW, Bucks   SU 9081   BM 98.7-12.17

   Found in a creek near Taplow
   Bibl: as Taplow 113 above
   Ferrule. Hollow cylinder, closed at one end. Opposed pegholes approximately half way along its length.
   118 mm x 16 mm diam.
                                                 Fig. 26

119.   TAPLOW, Bucks   SU 9081   BM 98.7-12.18

   Found in a creek near Taplow
   Bibl: as Taplow 113 above
   Ferrule, broken at one end. Hollow cylinder. Opposed pegholes.
   206 mm x 17 mm diam.
                                                 Fig. 26

120. TAPLOW, Bucks.   SU 9381   BM 1902.12-16.1

   From Burnham Brickfield
   Tip and edges of wings broken. String side loops. Narrow leaf-
   shaped blade with circular-section midrib. Casting flashes remain
   on sides of socket from loops to base of blade.
   106 mm x 16 mm   33 g
   Class IV   Fig. 4

121. TAPLOW, Bucks   SU 9082   BM.1093.6-23.1

   Found in Thames below Boulter's Lock
   Bibl: Read, 1903, 288; Clinch, 1905, 184; Shrubsole, 1906, 185;
   BM, 1920, 38
   Socket and one loop broken. String-type loop at base of, but separate
   from, blade. Blade rapier-shaped, with bevelled edges. Decoration
   comprises two pairs of conical gold studs on bottom part of blade;
   loops and blunt underside of blade are incised with v-shaped lines;
   pointillé outlining the junction of wings and midrib. Part of wooden
   shaft remains in socket.
   440 mm x 65 mm   360 g
   Class IV A   Fig. 12

122. TAPLOW, Bucks   SU 9082   BM Unregistered

   Tip only. Edges of blade bevelled. Circular-section midrib.
   62 mm x 30 mm
   Class V ?   Fig. 18

123. TAPLOW, Bucks   SU 9082   RM 136.61/1-2 (AL 8)

   From Taplow Mills (Thames) ex-Rutland Collection
   In two pieces, but almost complete. Tip bent. Opposed pegholes
   near socket mouth. Lanceolate blade, with bevelled edges and circular-
   section midrib. Long piece of wooden shaft remains.
   195 mm x 36 mm   132 g
   Class V   Fig. 18

124. TAPLOW, Bucks   SU 9082   BuCM 328.05

   From Taplow Mills
   Socket only. Small opposed pegholes.
   78 mm x 25 mm
   Class V   Fig. 18

125. TAPLOW, Bucks   c. SU 9082   PLU (Benson Coll.)

   Bibl: OS cards (no information given)

126. TAPLOW, Bucks   c. SU 9082   PLU (Benson Coll.)

   Bibl: OS cards (no information given)

127. THATCHAM, Berks   SU 530663   Newbury M. OA 261

Found while digging a hole for gravel west of Colthrop Mills.
Bibl: Peake, 1922, 130; Roskill, 1938, 19; Coghlan, 1966, 188
Lozenge-shaped basal loops. Leaf-shaped blade with bevelled edges.
Lozenge-section midrib.
213 mm x 43 mm   152 g
Class III A

128. THATCHAM, Berks   SU 530662   Newbury M. 1965

Found at edge of a commercial gravel pit just below ground surface.
Bibl: Coghlan, 1966, 189
'Found in extremely poor condition, and completely disintegrated on examination' (Coghlan, 1974, pers. comm.)

129. TILEHURST, Berks   SU 672755   RM 251.45

From Thames opposite Roebuck Inn
Bibl: Peake, 1931, 53
Part of socket damaged. String side loops. Leaf-shaped blade with circular-section midrib.
104 mm x 20 mm   31 g
Class IV   Fig. 4

130. TILEHURST, Berks   SU 672755   RM 254.45

From Thames opposite Roebuck Inn
Bibl: Peake, 1931, 235; Smallcombe and Collins, 1946, 65
Tip missing and part of midrib broken. Opposed pegholes. Leaf-shaped blade with offset base and bevelled edges. Circular-section midrib. Part of wooden shaft remains in socket.
157 mm x 51 mm   188 g
Class V   Fig. 19

131. TILEHURST, Berks   SU 668767   RM 62.48 (AL 5)

From Thames at Mapledurham Lock
Bibl: Shrubsole, 1906, 184; Manning and Leeds, 1921, 263
Lozenge-shaped basal loops. Leaf-shaped channelled blade with lozenge-section midrib. Part of wooden shaft remains in socket. Slight traces of casting flashes remain on one side of socket.
262 mm x 54 mm   240 g
Class III A   Fig.13

132. TILEHURST, Berks   SU 668767   RM 65.48 (AL 4)

From Thames at Mapledurham Lock
Bibl: Shrubsole, 1906, 184; Manning and Leeds, 1921, 263
Opposed pegholes. Elliptical blade with bevelled edges. Circular-section midrib. Part of wooden shaft remains in socket.
367 mm x 58 mm   410 g
Class V   Fig. 23

133. WALLINGFORD, Berks (Oxon)   SU 610894   RM 1270.64 (TCB 283)

From Thames below Wallingford Bridge
Bibl: BAJ, 1966, 75
Blade bent. Narrow basal loops. Triangular channelled blade, with lozenge-section midrib. Long piece of wooden shaft remains in socket.
328 mm x 43 mm   240 g
Class III A   Fig. 15

134. WALLINGFORD, Berks (Oxon)   SU 610894   Ash.M Pr. 374

From Thames, a few yards below Wallingford Bridge
Bibl: Akerman, 1869, 280; Evans, 1881, 249; Peake, 1931, 238; Leeds, 1939, 249
Socket slightly broken. Opposed pegholes with wooden peg going through remaining piece of shaft. Ogival blade with circular-section midrib.
182 mm x 39 mm
Class V   Fig. 21

135. WALLINGFORD, Berks (Oxon)   SU 610893   RM 1091.64 (TCB 277)

From Thames, below Wallingford Bridge
Bibl: Burgess, Coombs and Davies, 1972, 244
Opposed pegholes, with bronze peg with rounded ends <u>in situ</u>. Barbed blade with parallel sides. Ovate-section midrib. Socket does not extend into blade.
234 mm x 61 mm   290 g
Class VI   Fig. 24

136. .WALLINGFORD, Berks (Oxon)   SU 610894   PLU (formerly RM?)

In exposed section in bank of Thames with other artefacts (see Appendix II)
Bibl: Collins, 1949, 65
Socket and tip either of the same or different spearheads. Opposed pegholes. "Cast concentric ribbing round the mouth of the socket."
Class V

137. WENDLEBURY, Oxon   SP 559180   Ash. M 1926.232

Found in cutting for L & NW Railway
Bibl: Leeds, 1939, 247
In two pieces and slightly bent. Lozenge-shaped basal loops. Leaf-shaped channelled blade with lozenge-section midrib.
240 mm x 40 mm   193 g
Class III A   Fig. 13

138. OLD WINDSOR, Berks   c. SU 9974   RM 180.53

From the Thames between Old Windsor and Runnymede
Bibl: Palmer, 1860, 322; Peake, 1931, 246
Tip broken. Slightly bent and damaged. Narrow basal loops.

Triangular channelled blade with circular-section midrib.
414 mm x 56 mm 340 g
Class III A Fig. 16

139. OLD WINDSOR, Berks SU 993745 On loan to Windsor Guildhall (RM 252.63 (TCB 256))

Old Windsor Backwater, Thames
Bibl: <u>BAJ</u>, 1964, 108
Narrow basal loops. Triangular channelled blade with circular-section midrib.
356 mm x 50 mm
Class III A Fig. 15

140. OLD WINDSOR, Berks SU 9974 LM 49.107/878

From Thames. Formerly in Lloyd Coll., Richmond Library. String side loops. Leaf-shaped blade; lozenge-section midrib with ridge running along the top of it and extending onto socket. Casting flashes remain on socket.
100 mm x 17 mm
Class IV Fig. 8

141. OLD WINDSOR, Berks SU 9974 LM A19778

From Thames. ex-Greenwell Coll.
Ferrule. Hollow cylinder.
100 mm x 14 mm diam.

Fig. 26

142. OLD WINDSOR, Berks SU 967773 Windsor Guildhall R 147

Found near Windsor Bridge
Opposed pegholes near mouth of socket. Lanceolate blade with bevelled edges. Lozenge-section midrib. Slight traces of casting flashes remain on the sides of socket.
104 mm x 32 mm
Class V Fig. 22

143. OLD WINDSOR, Berks SU 9974 Windsor Guildhall R 150

ex-Rawlins Coll.
Socket mouth slightly damaged. String side loops. Leaf-shaped blade with lozenge-section midrib with ridge along the top of it and extending onto socket. Casting flashes remain on sides of socket.
101 mm x 21 mm
Class IV Fig. 8

144. OLD WINDSOR, Berks SU 9974 PLU (Wells Coll.)

Opposed pegholes. Slightly ogival blade with bevelled edge and circular-section midrib. Decorated with rows of incised lines around socket as far as pegholes, and dashed lines on level with pegholes.
98 mm x 37 mm 49.6 g
Class V Fig. 21

145. NEW WINDSOR, Berks   SU 9677   BM 96.1-21.1
    Found during dredging
    Bibl: Shrubsole, 1906, 180; Peake, 1931, 245
    Opposed pegholes near base of blade with a bronze peg in place.
    Also another small hole nearer mouth of socket, not in plane of wings.
    Lanceolate blade with offset base and circular-section midrib. Part
    of wooden shaft remains in socket.
    430 mm x 53 mm   390 g
    Class V   Fig. 19

146. NEW WINDSOR, Berks   SU 9677   Windsor Guildhall
                                                  W40.51
    Found on Isle of Sheppey, in a heap of ballast which originated from
    Windsor.
    Bibl: Grove, 1946, 67
    Broken into two pieces. String side loops. Blade irregularly shaped,
    possibly due to sharpening in antiquity. Lozenge-section midrib.
    Part of wooden shaft remains in socket. Casting flashes remain on
    sides of socket.
    158 mm x 21 mm
    Class IV   Fig. 8

147. WITTENHAM, Berks (Oxon) SU 568936   Ash. M 1921.77
    From Thames at Wittenham Lock
    Bibl: Peake, 1931, 52; Leeds, 1939, 247
    Narrow basal loops. Triangular channelled blade with circular-
    section midrib.
    262 mm x 42 mm   164 g
    Class III A   Fig. 17

YATTENDON, Berks   SU 562746   Newbury Museum
Found while digging foundations of Yattendon Court in 1878
The bronzes were all lying together and there was no sign of their having
been enclosed in any box or pot. Besides 28 spearheads and sockets the
hoard included:-

    1 flat axe
    3 palstaves
    2 socketed axes
    6 socketed gouges
    3 tanged knives
    2 socketed knives
    3 tanged chisels
    4 sword fragments
    1 chape
    3 pieces of flat bronze sheet
    1 'conical piece'
    1 perforated disc

The latest objects in the hoard belong to the middle of the Late Bronze Age. However, the flat axe is Early Bronze Age and the palstaves and five of the spearheads are probably Middle Bronze Age. It is, therefore, impossible to use this hoard, the only founder's hoard in the area, to date any of the spearheads. As is typical of founder's hoards, the bronzes are almost without exception in an extremely fragmentary state. This hoard containing mainly spearheads, but also axes, tools and ingot metal, falls between Burgess, Coombs and Davies' (1972, 229) two series of later Late Bronze Age or Ewart Park phase hoards, those in which spearheads are dominant, and the Carp's Tongue hoards, comprising mainly axes, tools and ingot metal. It includes both barbed spearheads typical of the Broadward tradition, and ogival spearheads typical of the Carp's Tongue Complex.

Bibl: Evans, 1879, 480; Evans, 1881, 466; Shrubsole, 1906, 182; Smith-Masters, 1929; Roskill, 1938; Coghlan, 1970; Burgess, Coombs and Davies, 1972, 236

The spearheads are as follows (Numbers are those given by Newbury Museum and published in Coghlan, 1970):-

Y 26 Socket only. Opposed pegholes
      55 mm   24 g
      Class V

Y 27 Blade only. Probably barbed with parallel sides. Ovate-section midrib.
      222 mm x 50 mm   185 g
      Class VI

Y 28 Edges of blade broken. Opposed pegholes. Lanceolate blade with circular-section midrib.
      167 mm x 37 mm   105 g
      Class V

Y 29 Blade only. Elliptical blade with bevelled edges. Circular-section midrib with semi-hollow socket.
      130 mm x 42 mm   70 g
      Class V

Y 30 Part of socket and tip of blade broken. Lanceolate blade with circular-section midrib.
      130 mm x 35 mm   62 g
      Class V

Y 31 Opposed pegholes. Lanceolate blade with circular-section midrib.
      162 mm x 36 mm   90 g
      Class V

Y 32 Blade only. Elliptical blade with bevelled edges. Circular-section midrib with semi-hollow socket.
      154 mm x 44 mm
      Class V

Y 33   Part of socket broken. Elliptical semi-hollow blade with bevelled
       edges and circular-section midrib.
       180 mm x 45 mm   125 g
       Class V

Y 34   Edges and tip of blade chipped away. Leaf-shaped basal loops.
       Leaf-shaped blade.
       168 mm x 23 mm   84 g
       Class III A

Y 35   Blade only. Lanceolate blade with circular-section midrib.
       115 mm x 31 mm   66 g
       Class V

Y 36   Blade only, the edges of which are broken. Lanceolate blade with
       circular-section midrib.
       87 mm x 31 mm   38 g
       Class V

Y 37   Part of socket missing. Leaf-shaped blade with bevelled edges and
       circular-section midrib. Probably side looped, but no traces of
       them remain.
       85 mm x 20 mm   21 g
       Class IV

Y 38   Small part of blade only. Thin ovate-section midrib.
       65 mm x 49 mm   47 g
       Class VI

Y 39   Tip of blade and mouth of socket broken. Opposed pegholes.
       Lanceolate blade with bevelled edges and circular-section midrib.
       136 mm x 33 mm   66 g
       Class V

Y 40   Mouth of socket broken, and edges of blade chipped away. Lozenge-
       shaped side loops. Leaf-shaped blade with bevelled edges. Sub-
       rectangular-section midrib.
       90 mm x 18 mm   22 g
       Class IV

Y 41   Small part of socket only. One peghole remains.
       53 mm   19 g
       Class V

Y 43   Mouth of socket and edges of blade broken. No loops or pegholes.
       Leaf-shaped blade with octagonal-section midrib and socket.
       135 mm x 30 mm   65 g

Y 44   Part of midrib only. Lozenge-shaped basal-loops - one only remains. Channelled blade with lozenge-section midrib.
106 mm   45 g
Class III A

Y 45   Tip of blade only. Blade has bevelled edges and circular-section midrib.
85 mm x 36 mm   46 g
Class V

Y 46   Tip and edges of blade broken. Opposed pegholes. Lanceolate blade with circular-section midrib.
117 mm x 25 mm   49 g
Class V

Y 47   Part of socket only. Opposed pegholes.
85 mm x 22 mm   72 g
Class V

Y 48   Blade only. Lanceolate lozenge-section blade.
82 mm x 30 mm   31 g
Class V ?

Y 49   Mouth of socket broken. Opposed pegholes. Ogival blade with bevelled edges and circular-section midrib.
112 mm x 30 mm   45 g
Class V - Carp's Tongue Complex

Y 50   Blade only. Elliptical blade with bevelled edges and circular-section midrib.
138 mm x 47 mm   70 g
Class V

Y 51   Socket and part of one loop only. Probably a narrow basal loop.
83 mm x 23 mm   46 g
Class III A

Y 52   Part of socket and tip of blade broken. Lanceolate blade with circular-section midrib.
114 mm x 35 mm   67 g
Class V

Y 53   Part of socket and tip of blade broken. Opposed pegholes. Lanceolate semi-hollow blade with bevelled edges. Circular-section midrib.
111 mm x 32 mm   62 g
Class V

Y 54   Part of blade missing. Opposed pegholes. Lanceolate blade with circular-section midrib.
100 mm x 39 mm   78 g
Class V

APPENDIX I

For ease of reference, the spearheads, followed by their catalogue number, are here grouped in Classes. Those with an asterisk were definitely found in the Thames or Kennet.

Class I - (Tanged)

Datchet 45*   Newbury 86

Class II - (End Looped)

Akeley 3

Class III - (Kite Bladed)

Akeley 2   Reading 98*

Class III A - (Basal Looped with Leaf-Shaped Blades)

Bray 19	Dorchester 54	Speen 106*
Bray 23	Eton 55*	Thatcham 127*
E. Challow 31	Marlow 79*	Tilehurst 131*
Clewer 32*	Sandford 99*	Wendlebury 137
Datchet 42*		

Class III A - (Basal Looped with Triangular Blades)

Caversham 30*	Hedsor 67*	Windsor 138*
Cookham 39*	Maidenhead 78*	Windsor 139*
Datchet 46*	Stratfield Mortimer 109*	Wittenham 147*
Datchet 47*	Wallingford 133*	

Class IV - (Leaf-Shaped Side-Looped)

Amerden 4*	Datchet 43*	N. Hinksey 68
Amerden 5*	Datchet 48*	N. Hinksey 69
Amersham 7	Eton 56*	Kintbury 71
Ashbury 9	Eton 57*	Littlemore 72
Aston 10	Eton 58*	Medmenham 80
Aylesbury 11	Eton 59*	Newbury 88
Burgesses Meadow 24	Fyfield 61*	Newbury 89
Burgesses Meadow 25	Hagbourne 62	Padworth 90
Burghfield 26*	Hagbourne 63	Princes Risborough 91
Burghfield 27*	Hagbourne 64	Princes Risborough 92
Burghfield 28	Hatford 64	Pusey 93
Cookham 35*	Hatford 65	Saunderton 100

Shifford 101* Standlake 108 Windsor 142*
Sonning 103 Taplow 120 Windsor 143
Sparsholt 104 Tilehurst 129* Windsor 146
Speen 105 Windsor 140*

Class IV A - (Rapier Bladed)

Taplow 121*

Class V - (Plain Pegged)

Abingdon 1* Datchet 52* Taplow 111*
Benson 12* Datchet 53* Taplow 112*
Bray 17* Eton 60* Taplow 113*
Bray 20* Headington 66 Taplow 114*
Bray 21 Maidenhead 73* Taplow 115*
Bray 22 Maidenhead 74* Taplow 116*
Burghfield 29* Maidenhead 75* Taplow 117*
Clewer 33* Maidenhead 76* Taplow 122
Cookham 34* Mollington 81 Taplow 123*
Cookham 36* Mollington 82 Taplow 124
Cookham 37* Mollington 83 Tilehurst 130*
Cookham 38* Mollington 84 Tilehurst 132*
Culham 41 Pusey 94 Wallingford 134*
Datchet 44 Reading 96 Wallingford 136*
Datchet 49* Reading 97 Windsor 144
Datchet 50* Sonning 102* Windsor 145*
Datchet 51* Taplow 110*

Class VI - (Barbed)

Bray 15* Maidenhead 77* Speen 107
Bray 16* Moulsford 85* Wallingford 135*
Bray 18

Ferrules

Amerden 6* Taplow 119* Windsor 141*
Taplow 118*

APPENDIX II

Notes on the Spearheads from Hagbourne Hill and Wallingford

(i) Hagbourne Hill (62-64)

A number of finds have been made on Hagbourne Hill, including three spearheads (62-64). The combined evidence for the finds is extremely confused and the following facts which emerge do not seem to correlate:-

- a). In 1861 a spearhead (62) was given to BM with other artefacts including bronze collars, discs, possibly coins, a socketed axe and certain La Tène objects.

- b). In 1862 two spearheads (63 and 64), one probably from the same mould as 62 were acquired by BM. They are said to have been found by the side of a skeleton on Hagbourne Hill in 1803.

- c). In 1803 Ebeneezer King recorded that a socketed axe, at least one spearhead, two horse bits no earlier than the first century B.C. (Harding, 1972, 91), a cast ring-headed pin, paralleled in the Iron Age Arras culture, and one gold or silver coin, either Gallo-Belgic or Roman, were found in a circular pit at the bottom of a rectangular pit on Hagbourne Hill (King, 1812, 348).

- d). In 1845 Jesse King exhibited "Roman and Romano-British" antiquities found in Berkshire at the British Archaeological Association, which included a "javelin head in bronze found with a skeleton at Hagbourne Hill" (King, 1845, 310).

- e). In 1939 seven or eight rectangular pits, apparently resembling that recorded by E. King, were found with some Iron Age pottery, during building work on Hagbourne Hill.

Harding (1972, 92) suggests, tentatively, that the site, and in particular the rectangular pits, may have been an Iron Age cemetery, bearing affinities with early La Tène sites in Champagne. If so, the spearhead found with a skeleton may represent the first use of the site as a cemetery.

Alternatively, the various accounts may indicate a number of separate finds which represent repeated use over several centuries of the site which is on the Icknield Way, overlooking the Thames Valley.

(ii) Wallingford (136)

In the winter of 1948-9, part of the Berkshire bank of the Thames at Wallingford collapsed, and the fresh exposure was found to be of considerable interest (Collins, 1949, 65). At a depth of about one metre below the surface, covered by pale brown alluvial soil, was a dark brown earthy deposit about 10 cm thick, which contained many animal bones, two fragments of human skull, bronzes and pottery.

The bronzes include a complete tanged chisel, a broken socketed sickle and two broken pieces of the same or different spearheads (Wallingford 136). Unfortunately I have been unable to examine it, but the socket is described as having cast concentric ribbing round the mouth, possibly in the same manner as Sonning (102), which may be of very late Bronze Age or early Iron Age date (see page 15 above).

The sherds of pottery are mostly of hard-baked thin ware, dark buff to black in colour, with a large amount of burnt flint gritting. One has diagonal slashings on the shoulder, while another has 'pie crusting' on the rim, and another has a rounded everted rim. All these are typical of the earliest phase of the Iron Age in the area (Harding, 1974, 144).

These finds are probably best interpreted as a settlement site, and rather than considering the bronzes as residual, on an Iron Age site, as Collins (1949, 66) did, they should, probably, be added to the growing body of evidence for the contemporaneity of the final phases of the Bronze Age and the earliest of the Iron Age.

Apart from the chronological interest of the site, it is of particular relevance to this study in the evidence it gives for the causes of metalwork being found in the Thames. Presumably part of this occupation deposit had been eroded into the Thames before it was observed, and presumably, too, had the section not been observed, the rest of it would also have been washed into the river. The pottery and bones, even if they had not been destroyed by the river action, would probably not have been noticed in subsequent dredging, whereas the bronzes may well have been.

How many other sites have been destroyed, unrecorded, in a similar way? And how many of the bronzes from the Thames came originally from similar sites?

BIBLIOGRAPHY

The following abbreviations are used in the bibliography:-

Ant	Antiquity
Ant J	Antiquaries Journal
Arch	Archaeologia
Arch J	Archaeological Journal
BAJ	Berkshire Archaeological Journal
BBOJ	Berkshire, Buckinghamshire and Oxfordshire Archaeological Journal
JBAA	Journal of the British Archaeological Association
PPS	Proceedings of the Prehistoric Society
PSA	Proceedings of the Society of Antiquaries of London
PSAS	Proceedings of the Society of Antiquaries of Scotland

Akerman, J. Y. (1869) Exhibit at the Society of Antiquaries PSA, IV, 280.

Allen, I. M., Britton, D. and Coghlan, H. H. (1971) Metallurgical reports of British and Irish Bronze Age implements and weapons in the Pitt-Rivers Museum.

Anati, E. (1964) The Camonica Valley.

Bartlett, J. E. and Hawkes, C. F. C. (1965) A Barbed Spearhead from North Ferriby, Yorkshire PPS, XXXI, 370-373.

Baynes, E. N. (1921) A Neolithic Bowl and other objects from the Thames at Hedsor near Cookham Ant J, I, 316-320.

Benson, D. and Miles, D. (1974) The Upper Thames Valley, an archaeological survey of the river gravels.

British Museum (1920) Bronze Age Guide.

Britton, D. (1960) Bronze Age Grave Groups and Hoards in the British Museum Inventaria Archaeologica, 8th Set, GB 48-54.

Britton, D. (1963) Traditions of Metalworking in the Late Neolithic and Early Bronze Age of Britain: Pt. I PPS, XXIX, 258-325.

Britton, D. (1968a) Late Bronze Age finds in the Heathery Burn Cave, Co. Durham Inventaria Archaeologia, 9th Set, GB 55.

Britton, D. (1968b) The Bronzes, in Cotton and Frere, 1968.

Brown, M. A. and Blin-Stoyle, A. E. (1959) A Sample Analysis of British Middle and Late Bronze Age materials using optical spectrometry PPS, XXV, 188-208.

Bunny, E. B. (1860) Exhibit to the British Archaeological Association JBAA, XVI, 322.

Burgess, C. B. (1968) Bronze Age Metalwork in Northern England c. 1000-700 B.C.

Burgess, C. B. (1968b) Bronze Age Dirks and Rapiers as illustrated by examples from Durham and Northumberland Trans Archit. Archaeol. Soc. Durham Northumberland, new ser. I, 3-26.

Burgess, C. B. (1969) The later Bronze Age in the British Isles and North-Western France Arch J, CXXV, 1-45.

Burgess, C. B. (1974) The Bronze Age, in Renfrew, C. (ed.) British Prehistory.

Burgess, C. B. (1976) The Gwithian mould and the forerunners of South Welsh axes (Appendix to J. V. S. Megaw, Gwithian, Cornwall - some notes on the evidence for Neolithic and Bronze Age settlement) in Burgess, C. B. and Miket, R. (ed.) Settlement and Economy in the Third and Second Millenia BC = B.A.R. 33, 69-75.

Burgess, C. B., Coombs, D. and Davies, D. G. (1972) The Broadward Complex and Barbed Spearheads, in Burgess, C. B. and Lynch, F. (ed.) Prehistoric Man in Wales and the West.

Burgess, C. B. and Cowen, J. D. (1972) The Ebnal Hoard and Early Bronze Age Metalworking Traditions, in Burgess, C. B. and Lynch, F. (ed.) Prehistoric Man in Wales and the West.

Butler, J. J. (1963) Bronze Age Connections across the North Sea Palaeohistoria, IX.

Clay, R. C. C. (1927) A Late Bronze Age Urnfield at Pokesdown, Hants. Ant J, VII, 465-484.

Clinch, G. (1905) Early Man, in Victoria County History of Buckinghamshire, Vol. I.

Coffey, G. (1896) Notes on the classification of spearheads of the Bronze Age found in Ireland Proc. Royal Irish Academy, III, 486-510.

Coghlan, H. H. (1951) Notes on the prehistoric metallurgy of copper and bronze in the Old World.

Coghlan, H. H. (1966) A Metallographic Examination of five spearheads from the collections of the Borough Museum, Newbury Berkshire Sibrium, VIII, 185-196.

Coghlan, H. H. (1970) A Report on the Hoard of Bronze Age Tools and Weapons from Yattendon, nr. Newbury, Berkshire.

Coghlan, H. H. and Raftery, J. (1961) Irish Prehistoric Casting Moulds Sibrium, VI, 223-244.

Coles, J. M. (1959-60) Scottish Late Bronze Age Metalwork PSAS, XCIII, 16-134.

Coles, J. M. (1963-4) Scottish Middle Bronze Age Metalwork PSAS, XCVII, 82-156.

Coles, J. M. (1965) The Ambleside hoard in its Bronze Age Context Trans. Cumberland and Westmorland Antiquarian and Archaeological Society, LXV, 43-47.

Coles, J. M. (1968-9) Scottish Early Bronze Age Metalwork PSAS, CI, 1-110.

Coles, J. M., Coutts, H. and Ryder, M. L. (1964) A Late Bronze Age Find from Pyotdykes, Angus PPS, XXX, 186-198.

Collins, A. E. P. (1949) Bronzes and Pottery from Wallingford BAJ, LI, 65.

Coombs, D. (1975) Bronze Age Weapon Hoards in Britain Archaeologica Atlantica, I, 49-81.

Coombs, D. (1975) The Dover Hoard bronze find - A Bronze Age Wreck? Archaeologica Atlantica, I, 2, 193-5.

Cotton, M. A. and Frere, S. S. (1968) Ivinghoe Beacon Excavations 1963-5 Records of Buckinghamshire, XVIII, 187-260.

Cowen, J. D. (1966) A Looped Spearhead from Millbourne Archaeologia Aeliana, XLIV, 232-235.

Crawford, O. G. S. and Wheeler, R. E. M. (1921) The Llynfawr and other hoards of the Bronze Age Arch, LXXXI, 133-8.

Curle, A. O. (1932-3) Account of Further Excavation in 1932 of the Prehistoric Township at Jarlshof, Shetland PSAS, LXVII, 82-136.

Davey, P. J. (1971) The Distribution of the Later Bronze Age Metalwork from Lincolnshire PPS, XXXVII, 96-111.

Davey, P. J. (1973) Bronze Age Metalwork from Lincolnshire Arch, CIV, 51-127.

Davey, P. J. and Knowles, G. C. (1971) The Appleby Hoard Arch J, CXXII, 154-161.

Davies, D. G. (1967) The Guilsfield hoard; a reconsideration Ant J, XLVII, 95-108.

Day, F. (1880-4) The Fishes of Great Britain and Ireland.

Eogan, G. (1964) The Later Bronze Age in Ireland in the light of recent research PPS, XXX, 268-351.

Evans, A. (1908) Discussion at Society of Antiquaries PSA, XXII, 121-129.

Evans, E. E. (1933) The Bronze Spearhead in Great Britain and Ireland Arch, LXXXIII, 187-202.

Evans, J. (1873) The Bronze Period PSA, V, 392-412.

Evans, J. (1879) A hoard of bronze antiquities found in Berkshire PSA, VII, 480-5.

Evans, J. (1881) Ancient Bronze Implements of Great Britain and Ireland.

Farley, M. (1972) A Bronze Spearhead from Princes Risborough Records of Buckinghamshire, XIX, 215.

Fitzstephen, W. (1183) Descriptio Londiniae.

Franks, A. W. (1865) Exhibit at Society of Antiquaries PSA, III, 166.

Gerloff, S. (1975) The Early Bronze Age Daggers in Great Britain.

Greenwell, W. and Brewis, W. P. (1909) The Origin, Evolution and Classification of the Bronze Spearhead in Great Britain and Ireland Arch, LXI, 439 ff.

Grove, L. R. A. (1946) A Bronze Spearhead from Windsor, Berkshire BAJ, IL, 67.

Grove, L. R. A. (1953) A Bronze Spearhead from Caversham BAJ, LIII, 118-9.

Harding, D. W. (1972) The Iron Age in the Upper Thames Basin.

Harding, D. W. (1974) The Iron Age in Lowland Britain.

Hawkes, C. F. C. (1941) The Looped and Leaf-Shaped Spearhead PPS, VII, 128-131.

Hawkes, C. F. C. (1955) Grave Groups and Hoards of the British Bronze Age Inventaria Archaeologica, 1st Set, GB 1-8.

Hawkes, C. F. C. and Smith, M. A. (1955) Bronze Age Hoards in the British Museum Inventaria Archaeologica, 2nd Set GB 9-13.

Hewett, H. J. (1902) Note BBOJ, VIII, 31.

Hodges, H. W. M. (1954) Studies in the Late Bronze Age in Ireland: 1, Stone and Clay Moulds and Wooden Models for Bronze Implements Ulster Journal of Archaeology, XVII, 62 ff.

Hodges, H. W. M. (1957) Studies in the Late Bronze Age in Ireland: 3, The Hoards of Bronze Implements Ulster Journal of Archaeology, XX, 51 ff.

Jope, E. M. (1961) Daggers of the Early Iron Age in Britain, PPS, XXVII, 307-343.

Kennet, D. H. (1969) The New Bradwell Late Bronze Age Hoard Journal Northampton Museum and Art Gallery, VI, 3-7.

King, E. (1812) A Description of Antiquities on Hagbourne Hill Arch, XVI, 348-9.

King, J. (1845) Note JBAA, I, 310.

Knight, R. W., Browne, C. and Grinsell, L. V. (1972) Prehistoric Skeletons from Tormarton Trans. Bristol and Gloucestershire Arch. Journal, XCI, 14-17.

Leeds, E. T. (1916) Two Bronze Age Hoards from Oxford PSA, XXXVIII, 147-153.

Leeds, E. T. (1939) Early Man, in Victoria County History of Oxfordshire, Vol. I.

Longmaid, N. (1966) *Bronze Age Metalwork in Norwich Castle Museum.*

Lowery, P., Savage, R. and Wilkins, R. (1971) Scriber, Graver, Scorper, Tracer: notes on Experiments in Bronze-Working Techniques *PPS,* XXXVII, 167-182.

Manning, P. (1898) Note *BBOJ,* IV, 18.

Manning, P. and Leeds, E. T. (1921) An Archaeological Survey of Oxfordshire *Arch,* LXXI, 227-265.

Mariën, M. E. (1958) *Trouvailles du Champ d'Urnes et des Tombelles hallstattienes de Court-Saint-Etienne.*

Moore, C. N. and Rowlands, M. (1972) *Bronze Age Metalwork in Salisbury Museum.*

Palmer, S. (1860) Exhibit to British Archaeological Association *JBAA,* XVI, 322.

Palmer, S. (1873) Exhibit at Society of Antiquaries *PSA,* V, 429.

Peake, H. (1922) Archaeological Finds in the Kennet Gravels near Newbury *Ant. J,* II, 125-130.

Peake, H. (1931) *The Archaeology of Berkshire.*

Powell, T. G. E. (1948) A Late Bronze Age Hoard from Welby, Leics. *Arch J,* CV, 27-40.

Read, (1903) Note *BBOJ,* IX, 87.

Roskill, V. (1938) Bronze Implements of the Newbury Region *Trans. Newbury and District Field Club,* VIII, 1-20.

Rowlands, M. J. (1976) *The Organization of Middle Bronze Age Metalworking* B.A.R. 31.

Rutland, R. A. and Greenaway, J. A. (1970) Archaeological Notes from Reading Museum *BAJ,* LXV, 53-60.

Savory, H. (1958) The Late Bronze Age in Wales *Archaeologia Cambrensis* CVII, 28-34.

Shrubsole, O. A. (1906) Early Man, in *Victoria County History of Berkshire,* Vol. I.

Smallcombe, W. A. and Collins, A. E. P. (1946) The Late George W. Smith of Reading *BAJ,* IL, 62-66.

Smith, M. A. (1959a) Some Somerset hoards and their place in the Middle Bronze Age of Southern Britain *PPS,* XXV, 144-187.

Smith, M. A. (1959b) Middle Bronze Age hoards from Southern England *Inventaria Archaeologica,* 7th Set, GB 42-47.

Smith-Masters, J. E. (1929) *Yattendon and its Church.*

Smith, W. J. B. (1854) Antiquities and Works of Art Described *Arch J,* XI, 186.

Smith, W. J. B. (1861)   Exhibit at The Archaeological Institute   <u>Arch J,</u> XVIII, 161.

Smith, W. J. B. (1873)   Exhibit to Society of Antiquaries   <u>PSA,</u> V, 430.

Tucker, C. (1867)   Notes on antiquities of bronze found in Devonshire   <u>Arch J,</u> XXIV, 110-122.

Tylecote, R. (1962)   <u>Metallurgy in Archaeology.</u>

Underhill, F. M. (1938)   Recent Antiquarian Discoveries (II)   <u>BAJ,</u> XLII, 20-28.

Underhill, F. M. (1946)   Notes on Recent Archaeological Discoveries in Berkshire   <u>BAJ,</u> IL, 49-61.

Wheeler, R. E. M.   (1921)   The Penard Hoard   <u>Arch,</u> LXXI, 138.

Wheeler, R. E. M. (1929)   Old England, Brentford   <u>Antiquity,</u> III, 20-32.

Wilde, W. (1861)   <u>Catalogue of the Antiquities of Bronze in the Museum of the Royal Irish Academy.</u>

Wymer, J. (1958)   Archaeological Notes from Reading Museum   <u>BAJ,</u> LVI, 54-59.

NOTES ON THE FIGURES AND PLATES

All the spearheads from Berkshire, Buckinghamshire and Oxfordshire, the present location of which is now known, and those now missing, but illustrated elsewhere, are drawn here, except for five in Newbury Museum, where it was not possible to draw them, and the Yattendon and Mollington hoards which have been recently published (Burgess, Coombs and Davies, 1972). Most of the spearheads which are now lost are recorded in the Bronze Implements Card Catalogue, housed in the British Museum, and are accompanied by illustrations of varying quality; these have been copied without any attempt, which would inevitably be inaccurate, at uniformity in shading and sections.

All the other spearheads are from my own drawings, and the following conventions have been used:- each spearhead is illustrated in front and side view. A section across the blade, at a position marked -   - is drawn above the front view. Where the internal section, whether hollow or solid, could be examined, this is shown. In many cases, however, the socket was found to be blocked either with the remains of wood from the shaft, or with sand and mud; in such cases the section contains a ?. Wherever it was possible to determine the extent of the socket the symbol π has been drawn opposite the point where the socket ends. A second section below the front view in every case shows the diameter and thickness of the socket mouth. Where this is broken, a dashed line -------- has been used to show the hypothetical shape of the socket mouth. The number beside each spearhead refers to its number in the catalogue.

THE SCALE ON ALL ILLUSTRATIONS COMPRISES CENTIMETRE DIVISIONS

Due to the great variation in size between the different classes of spearheads, Early Bronze Age, Kite-Bladed, and side-looped leaf-shaped spearheads, and Ferrules are illustrated at half of their full size, while basal-looped, pegged and barbed spearheads are shown at 1:3.

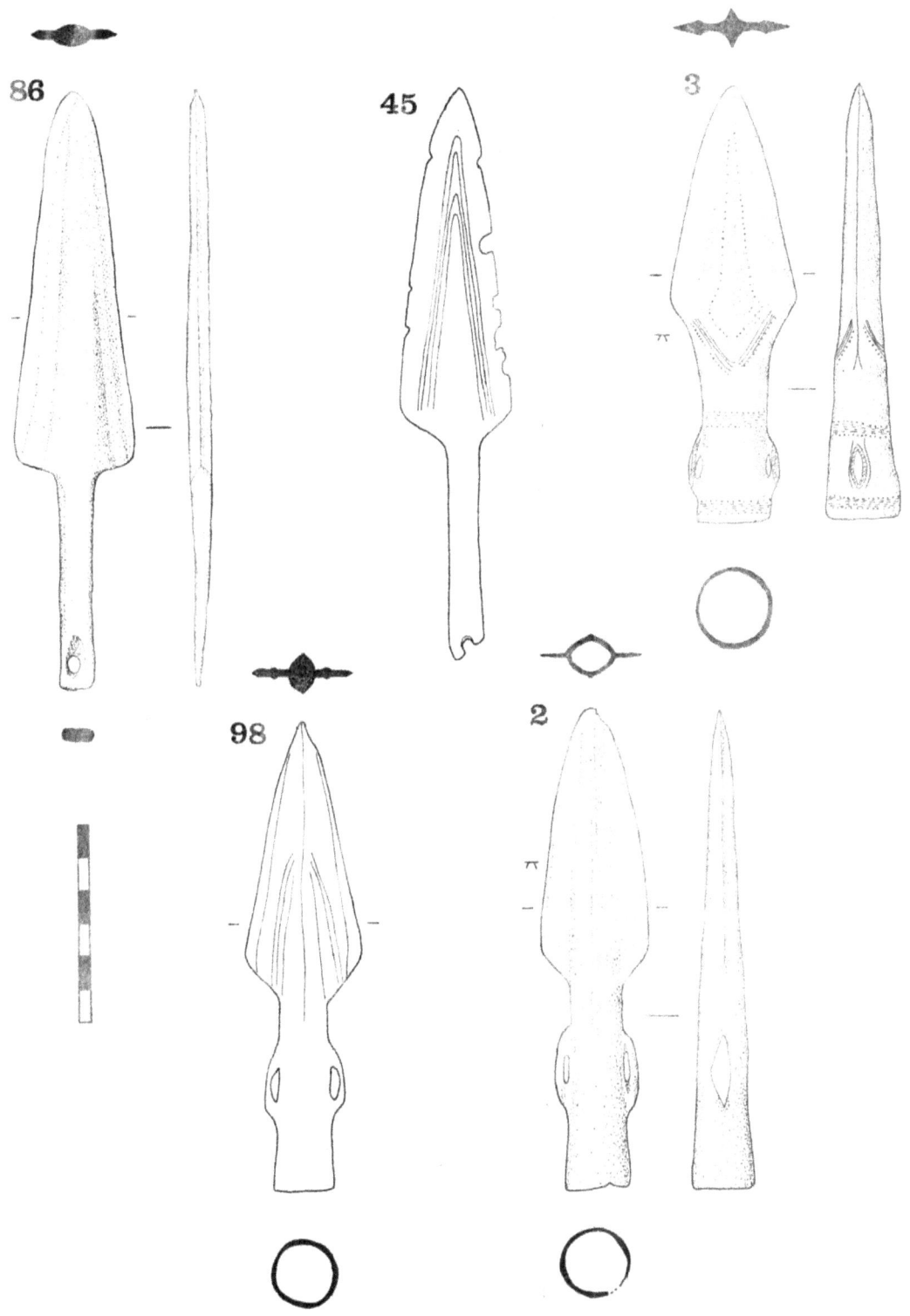

Fig. 3　EBA and Kite-Bladed Spearheads

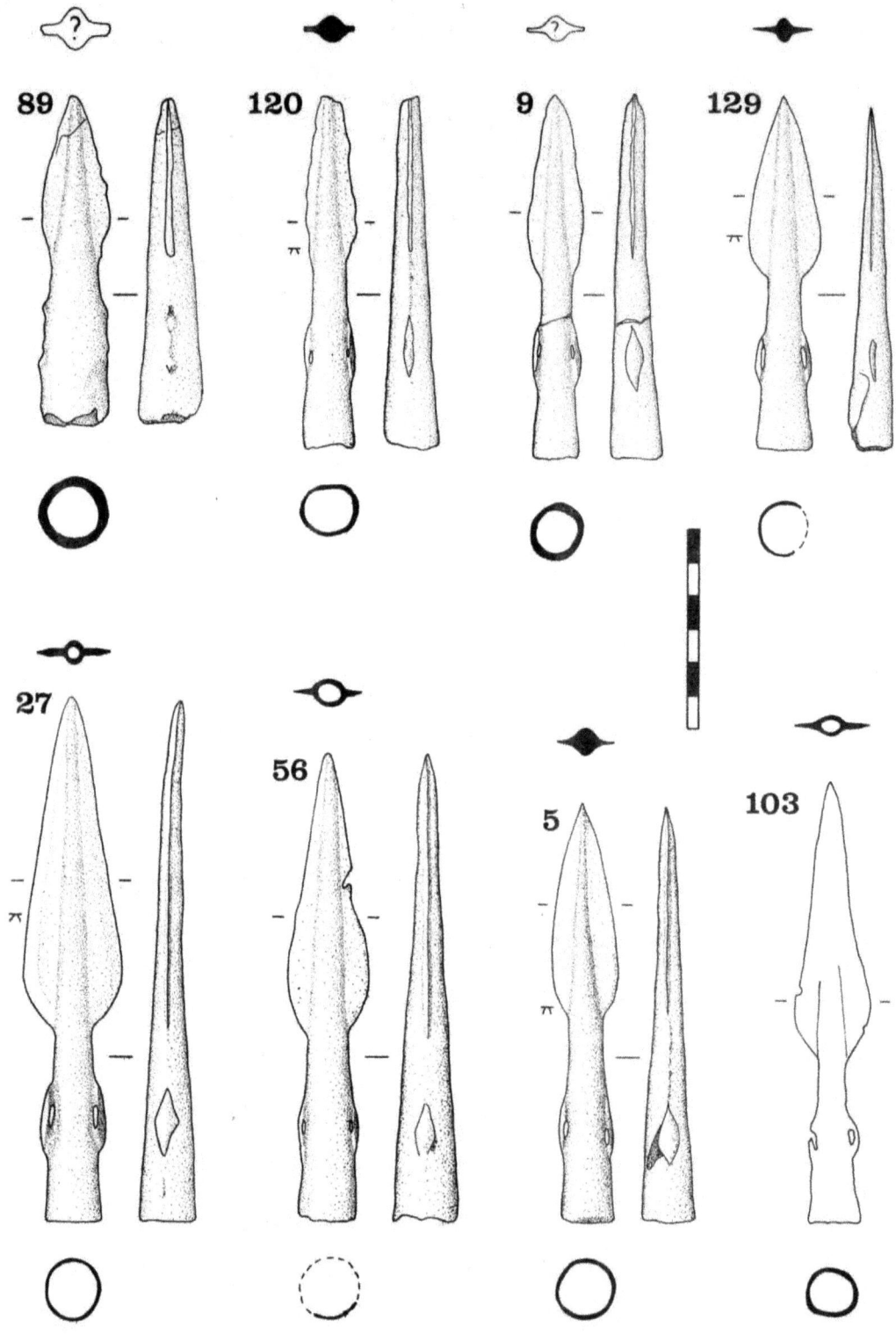

Fig. 4 Side-Looped Spearheads

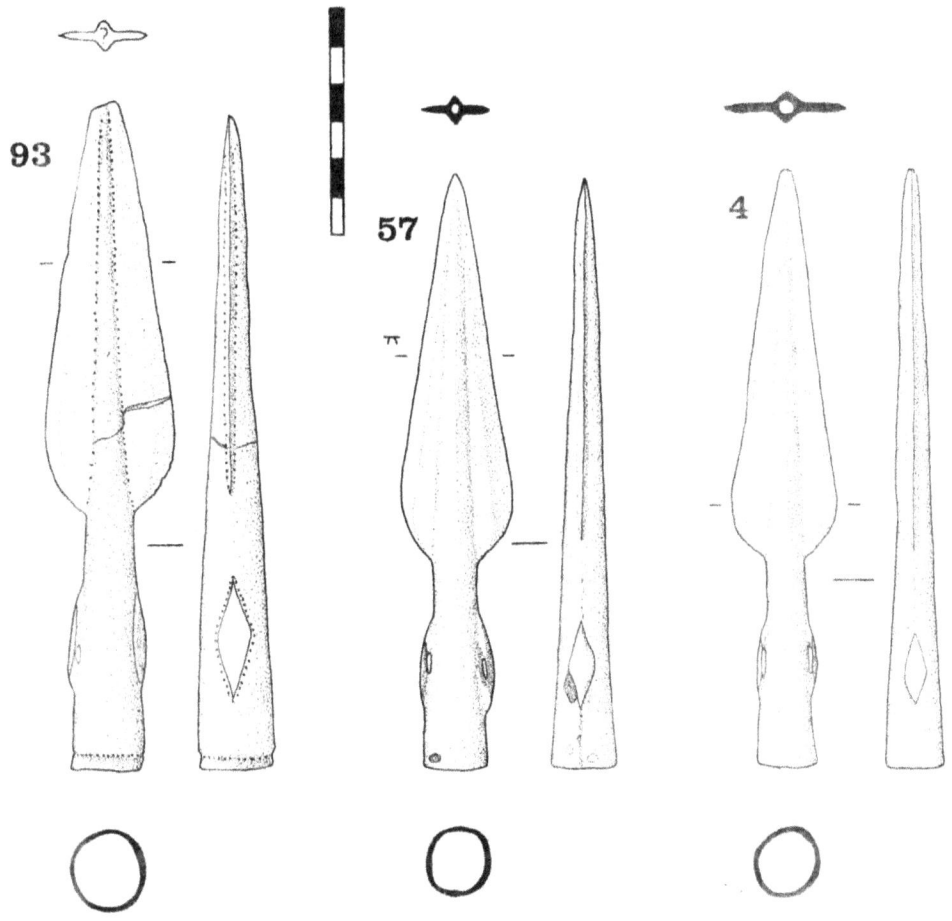

Fig. 5 Side-Looped Spearheads

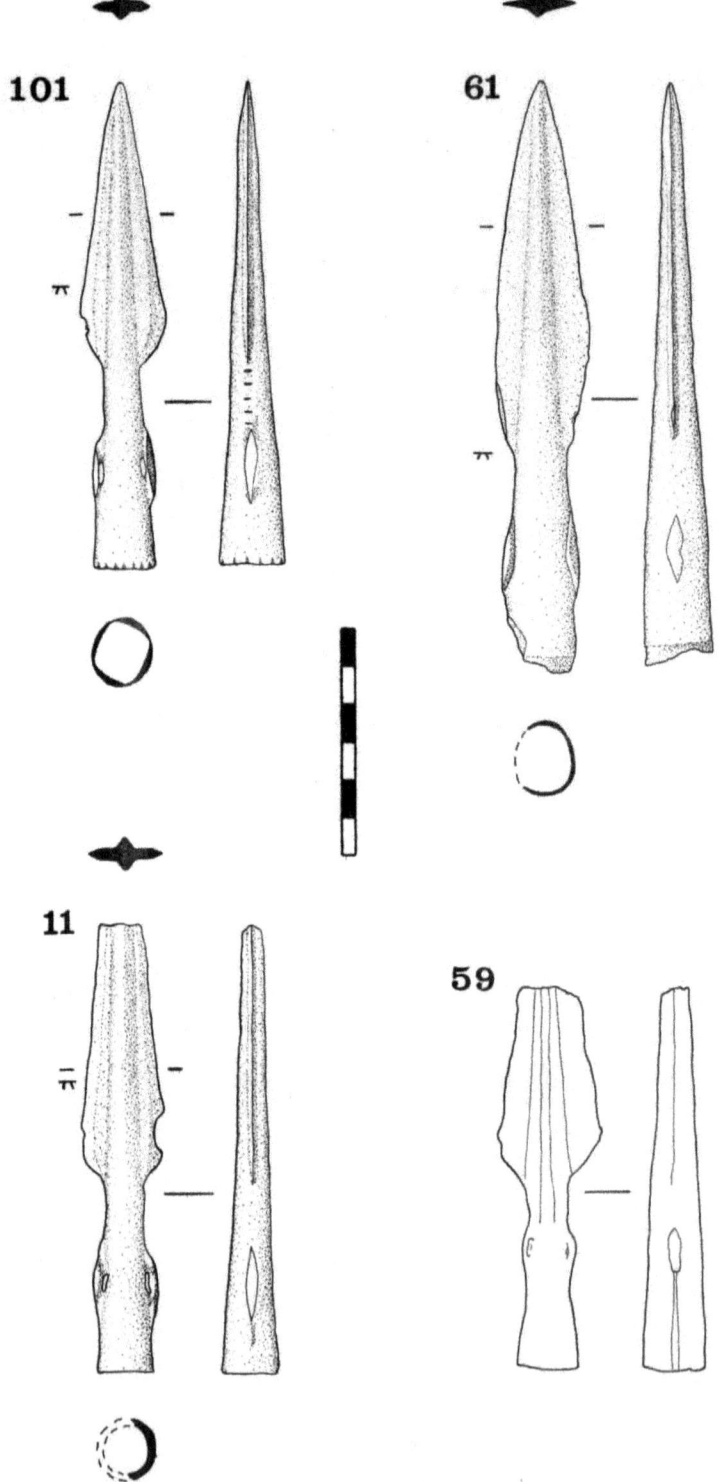

Fig. 6　Side-Looped　Spearheads

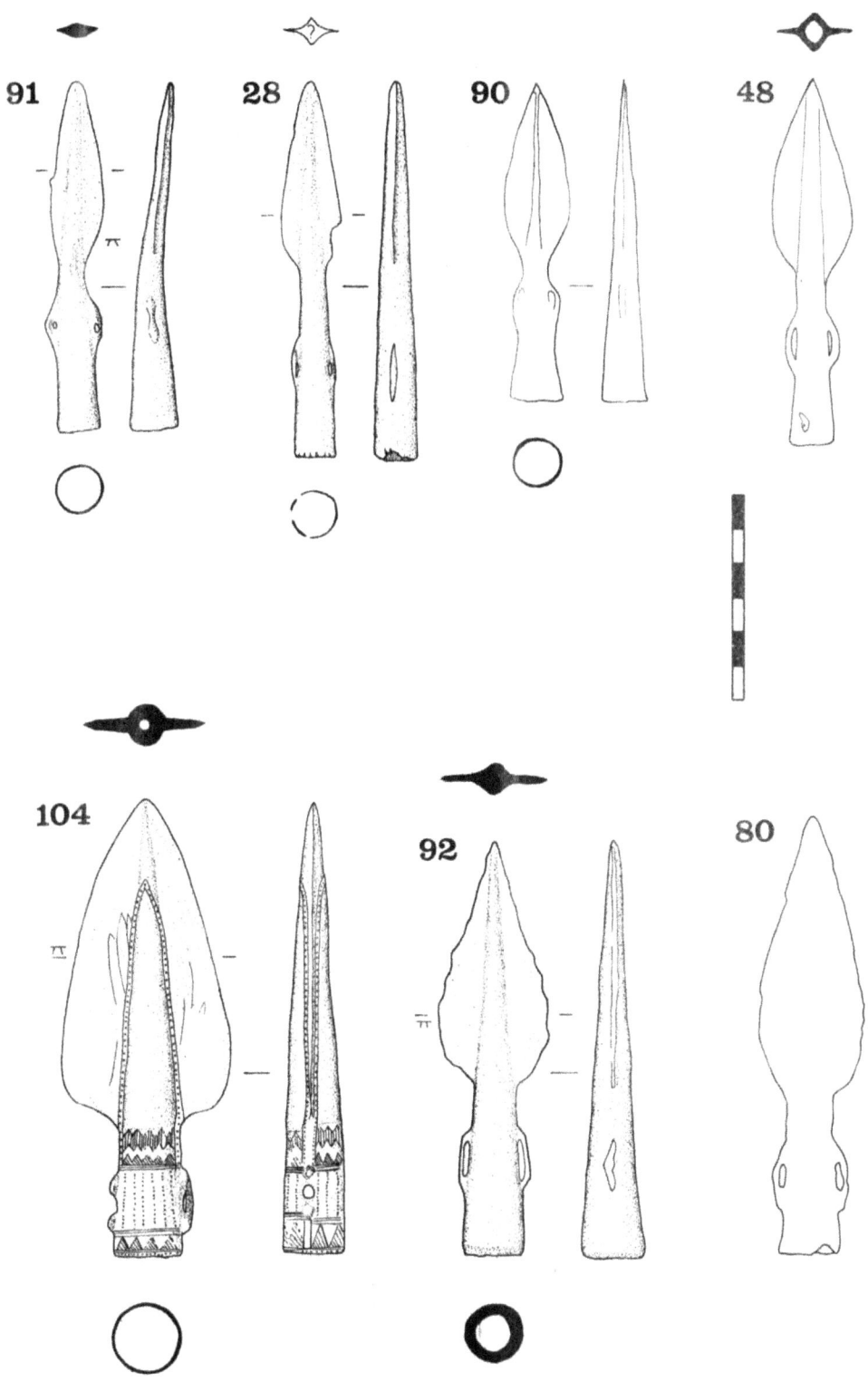

Fig. 7 Side-Looped Spearheads

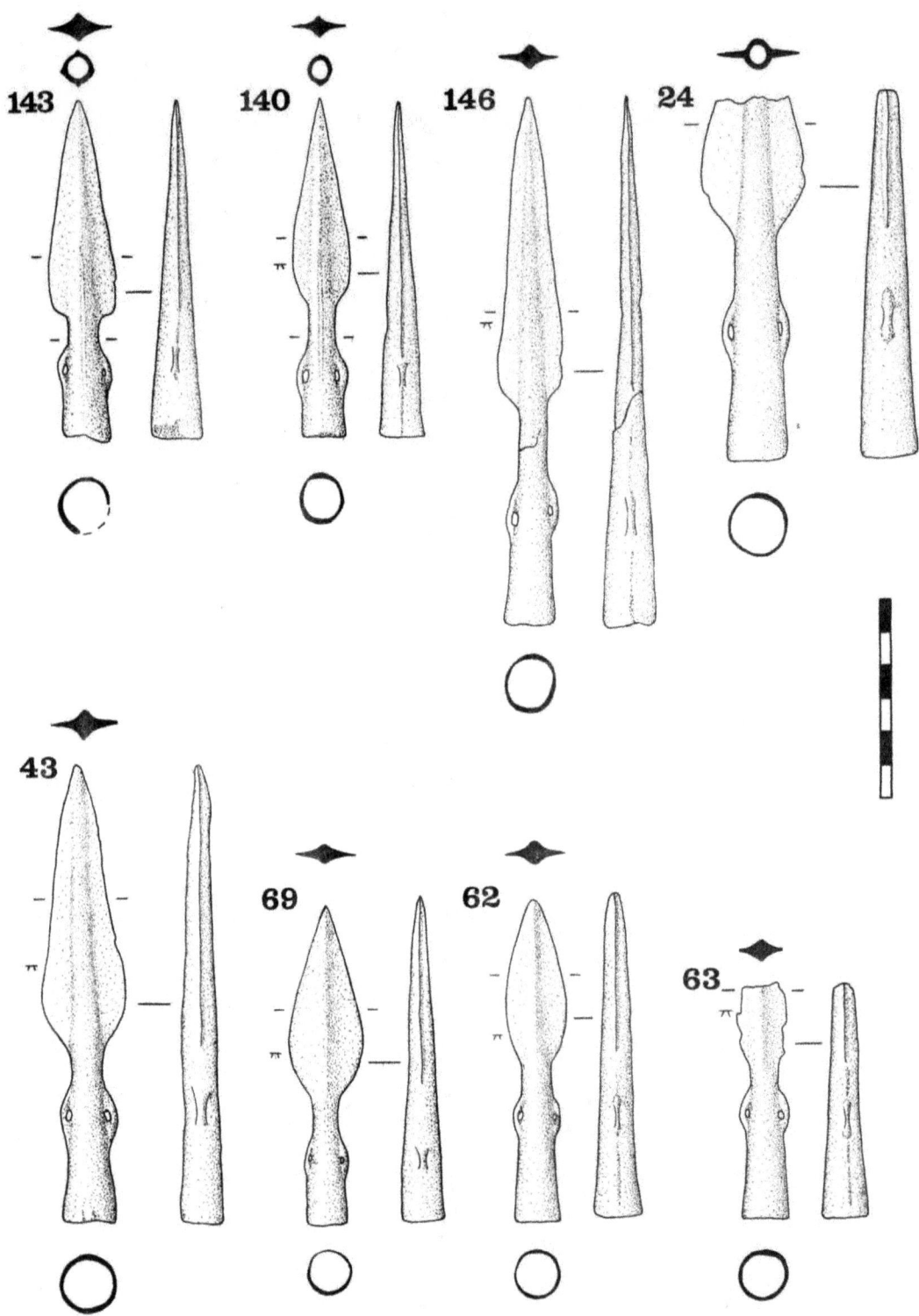

Fig. 8 Side-Looped Spearheads

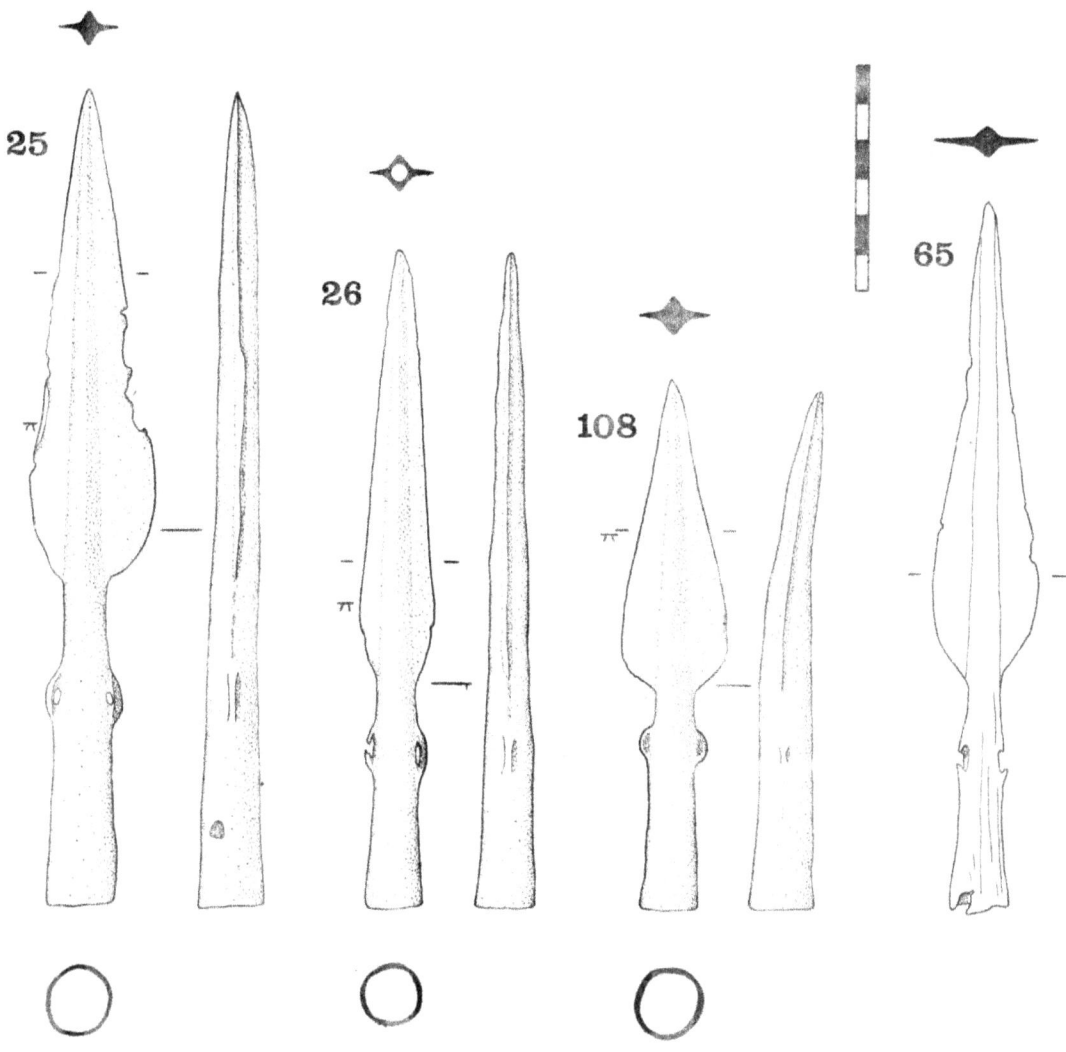

Fig. 9 Side-Looped Spearheads

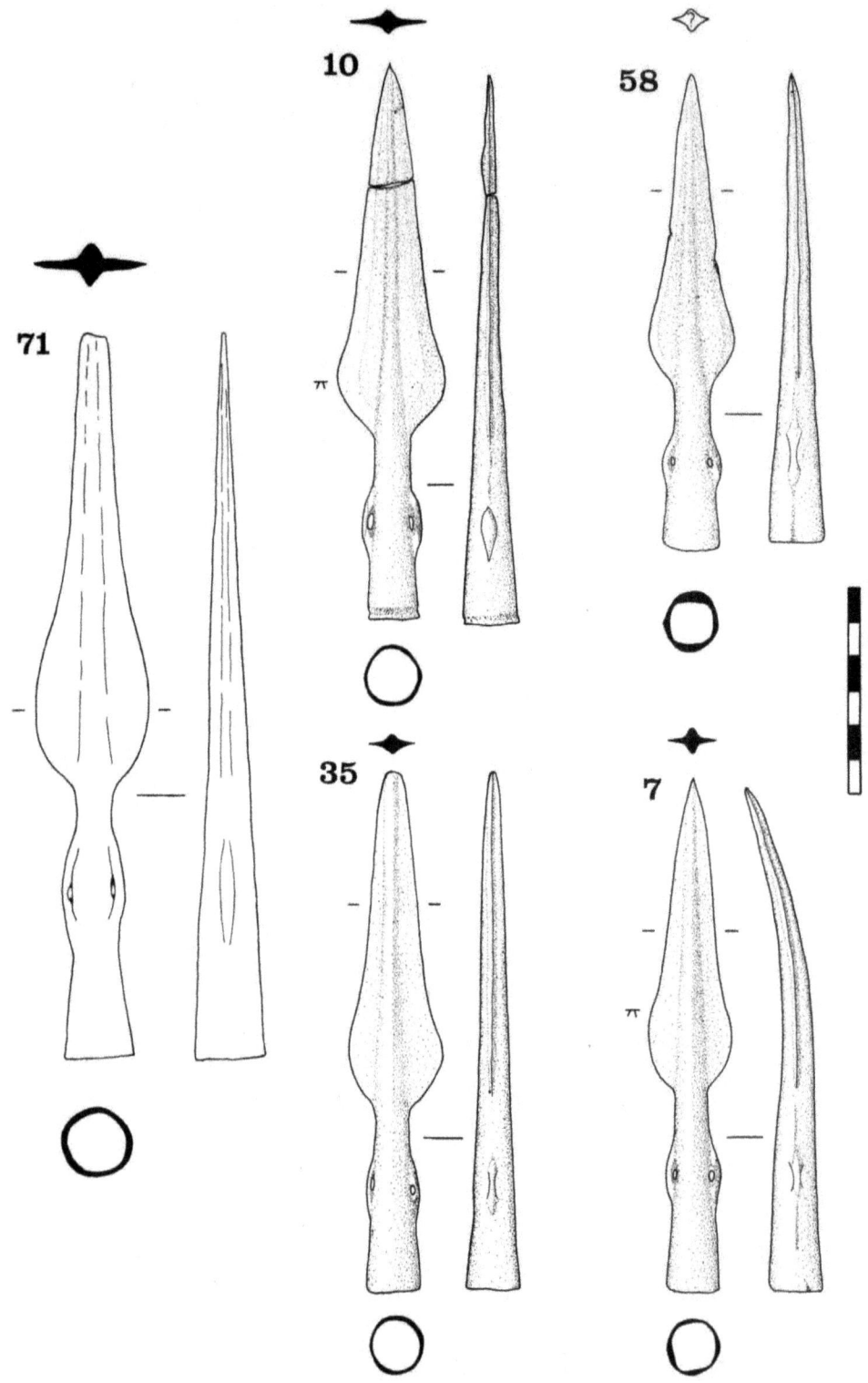

Fig. 10 Side-Looped Spearheads

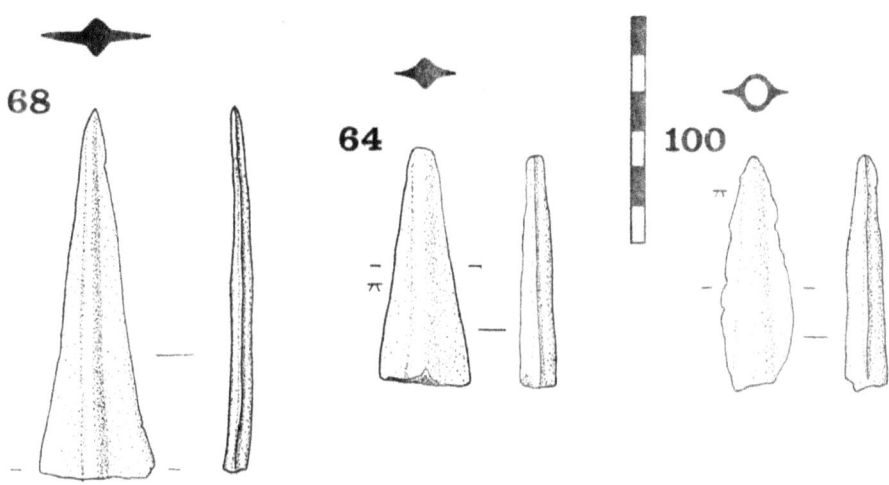

Fig. 11   Side-Looped Spearheads

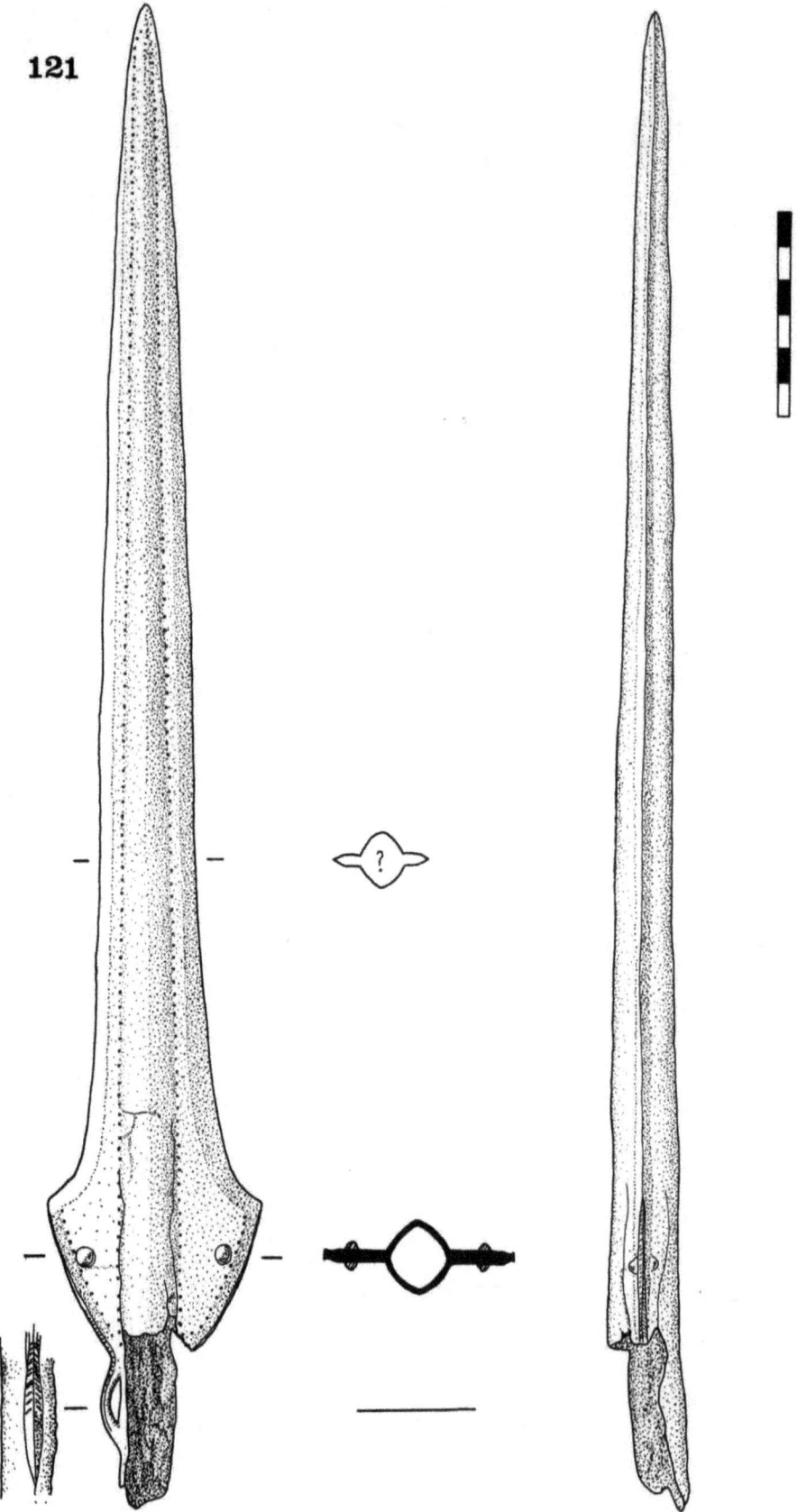

Fig. 12 Rapier-Bladed Spearhead

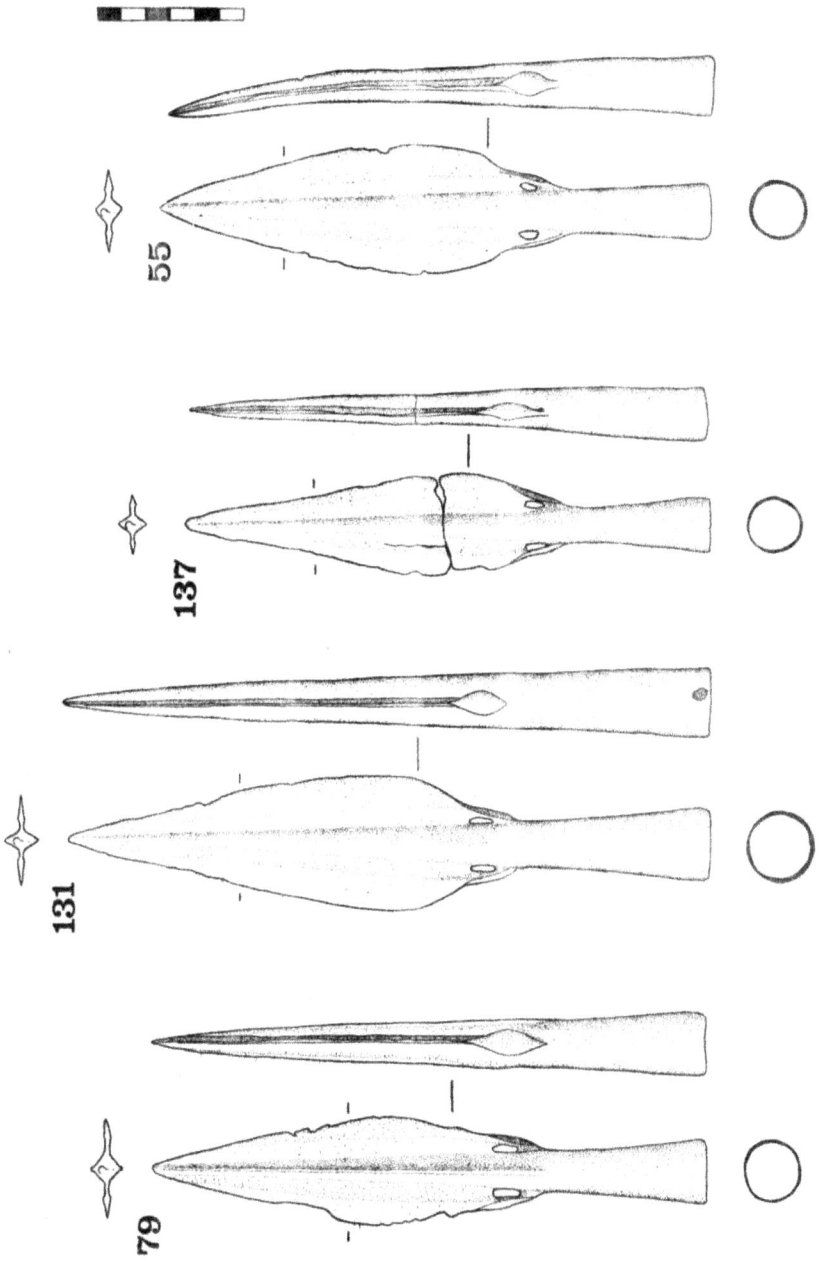

Fig. 13 Leaf-Shaped Basal-Looped Spearheads

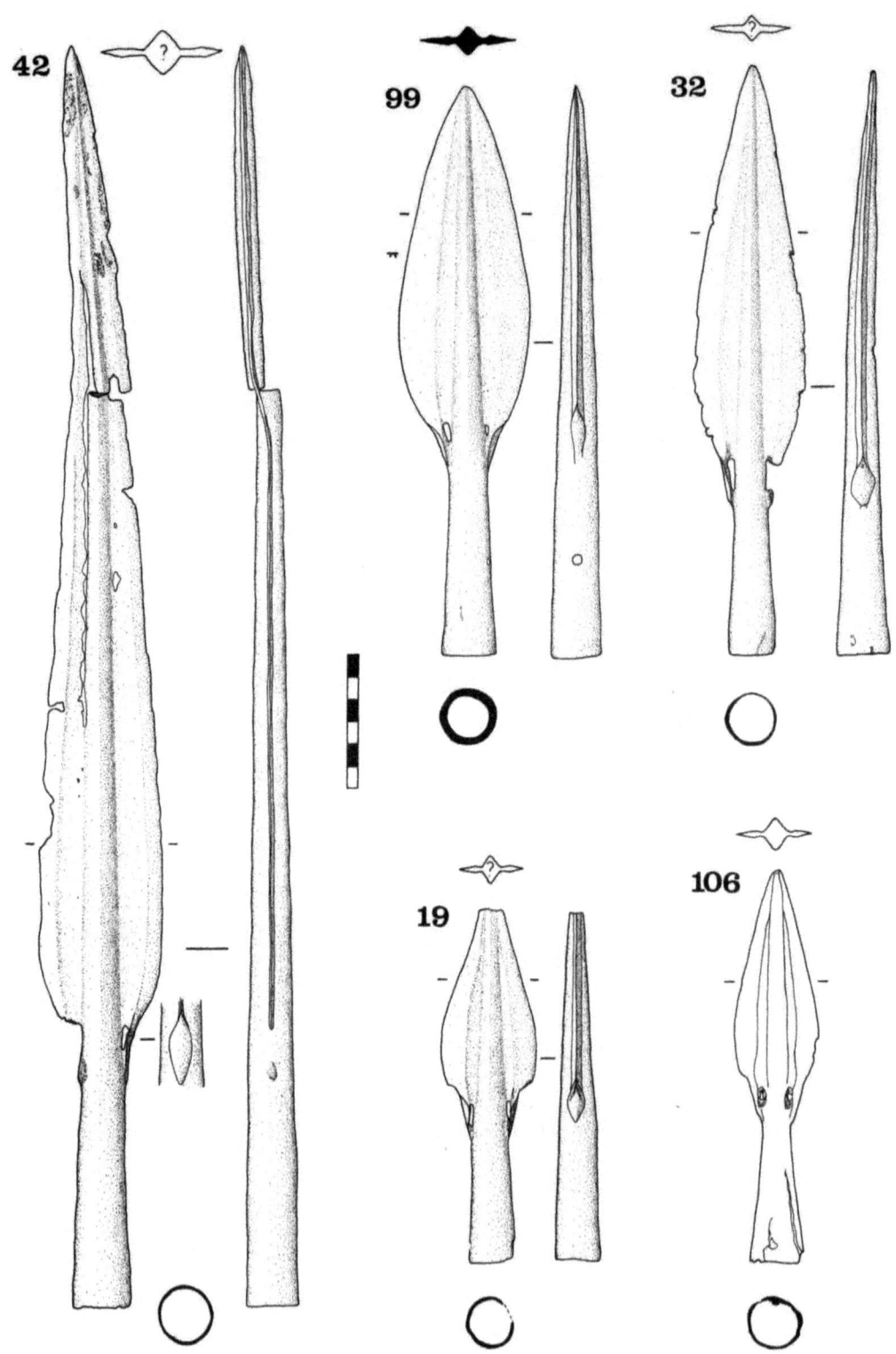

Fig. 14   Leaf-Shaped Basal-Looped Spearheads

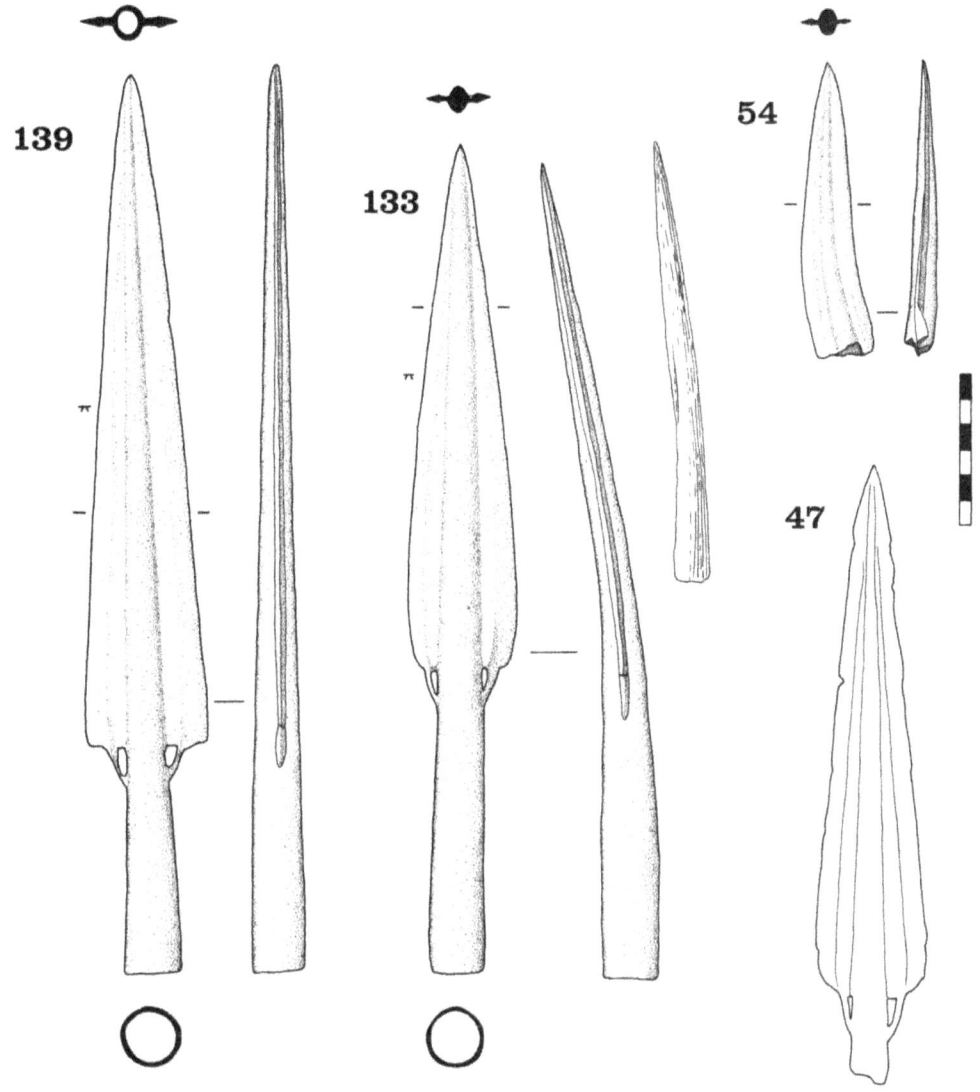

Fig. 15 Triangular-Bladed Basal-Looped Spearheads

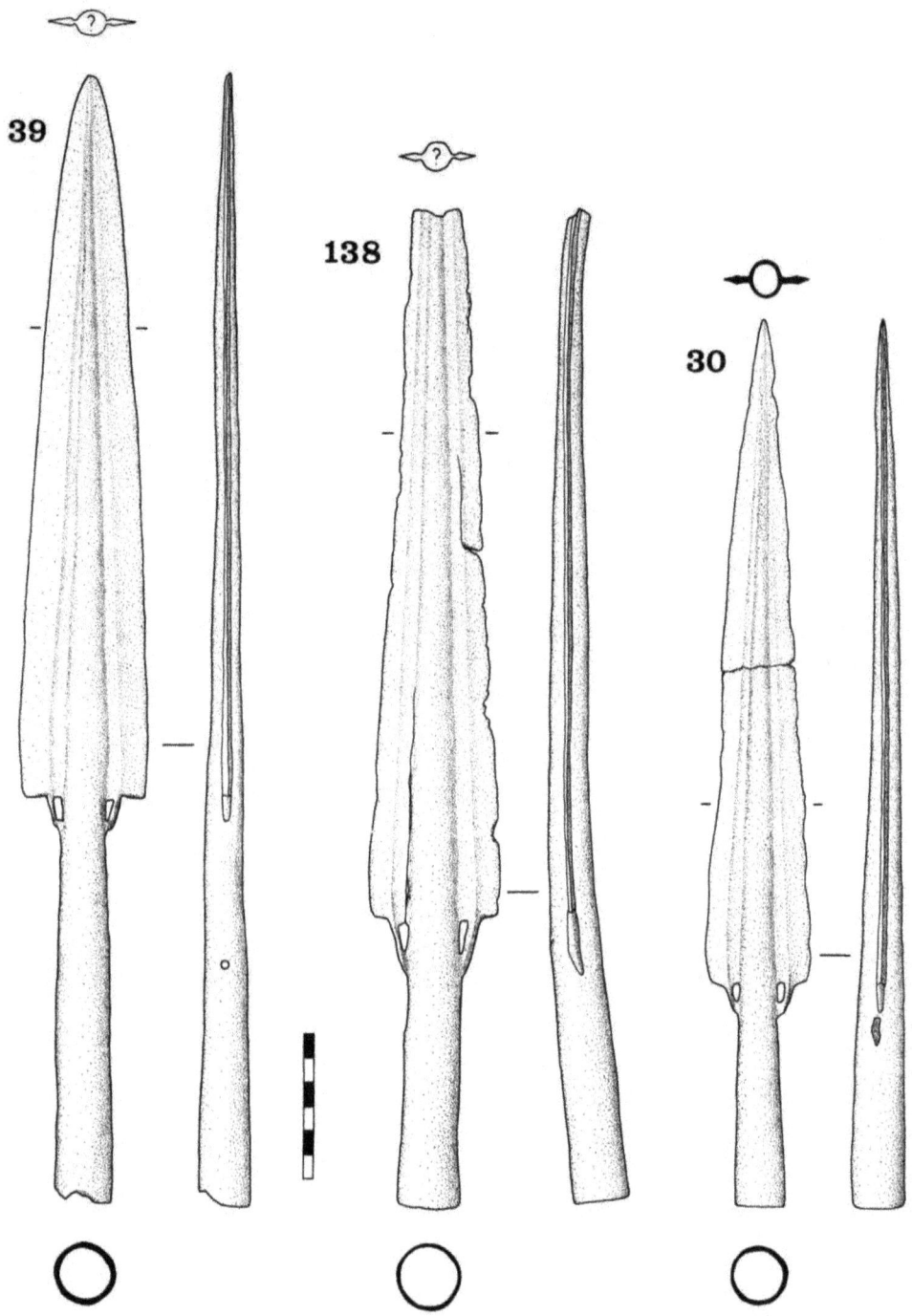

Fig. 16 Triangular-Bladed Basal-Looped Spearheads

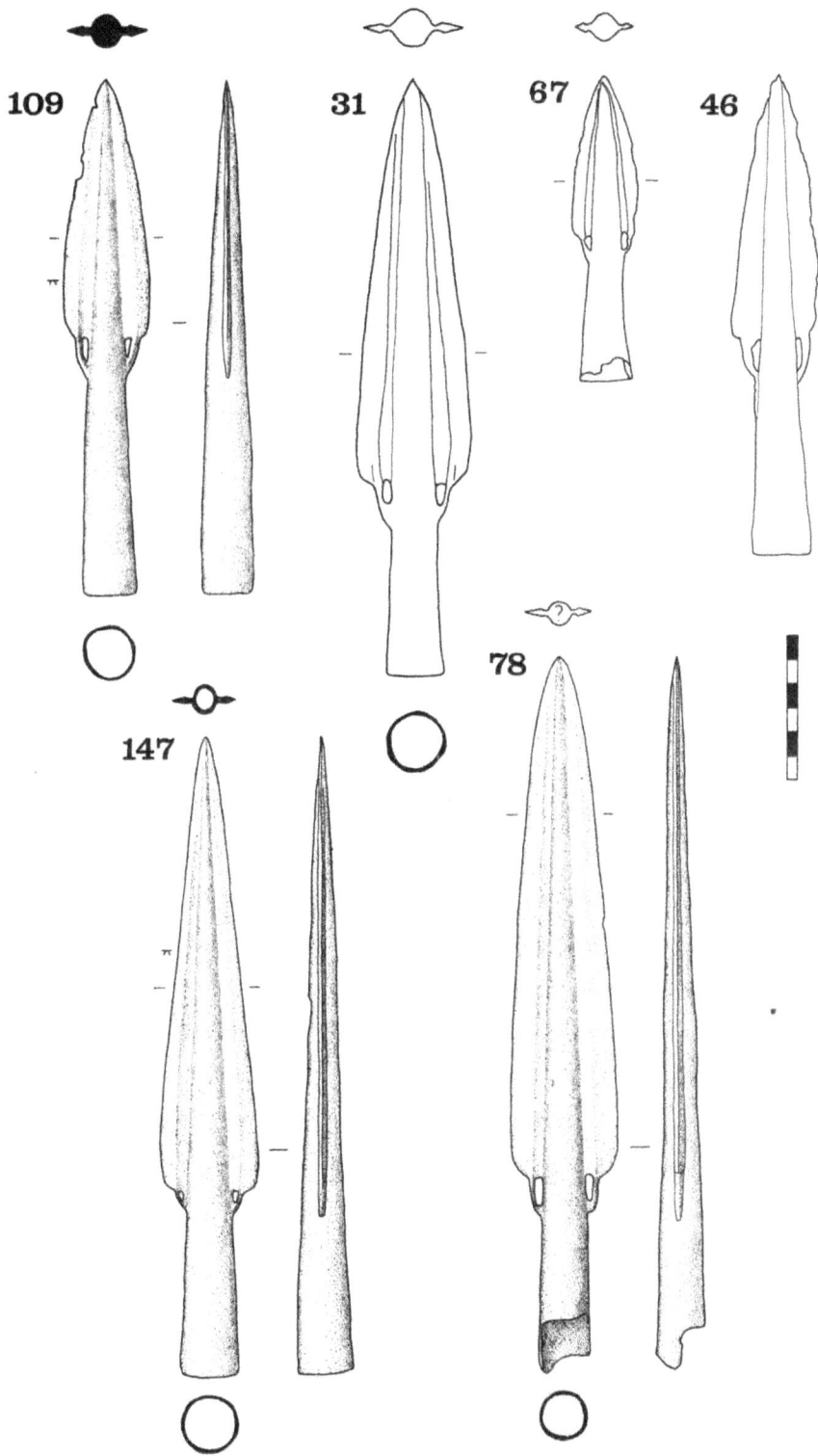

Fig. 17 Triangular-Bladed Basal-Looped Spearheads

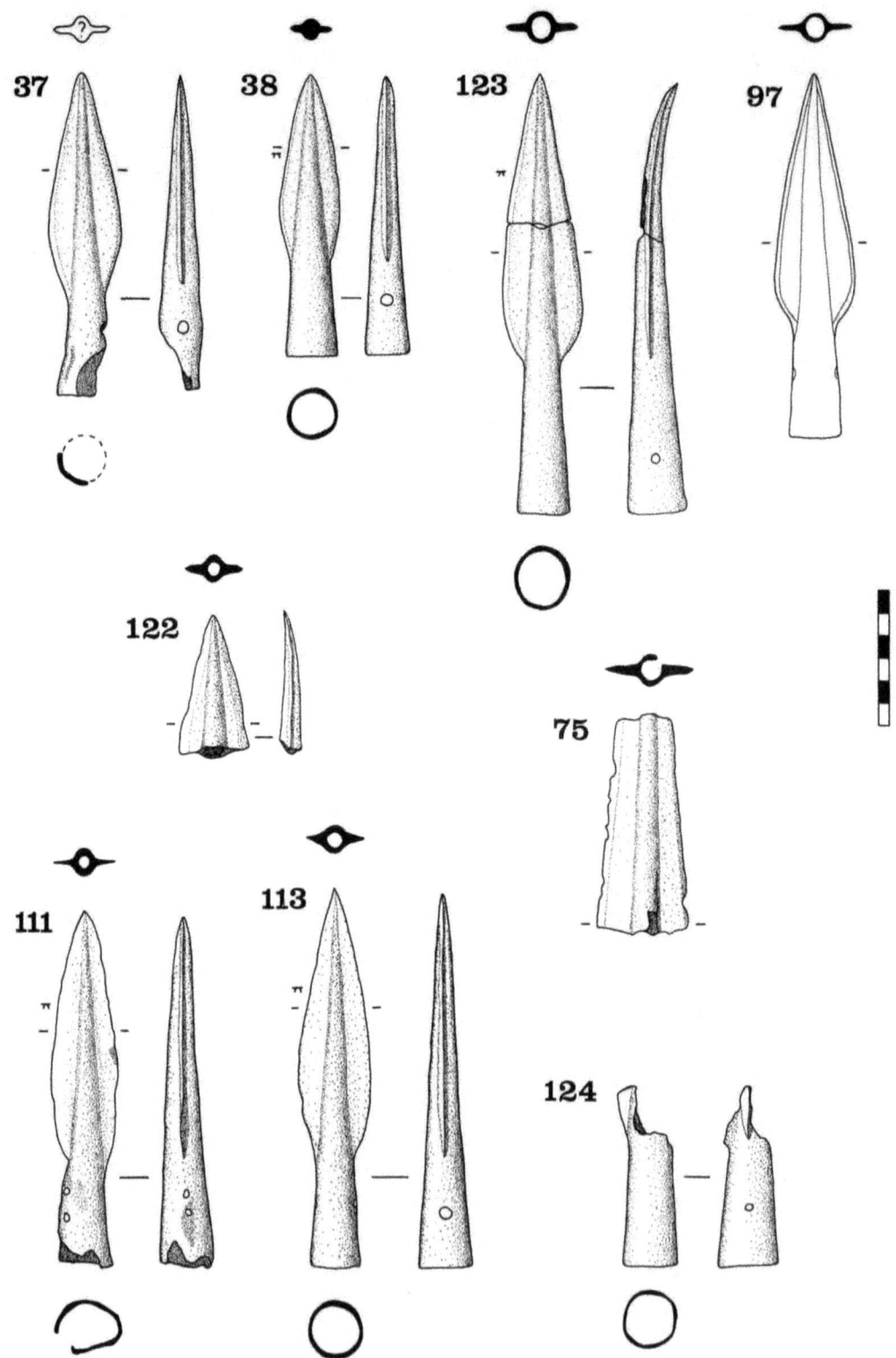

Fig. 18 Pegged Leaf-Shaped Spearheads

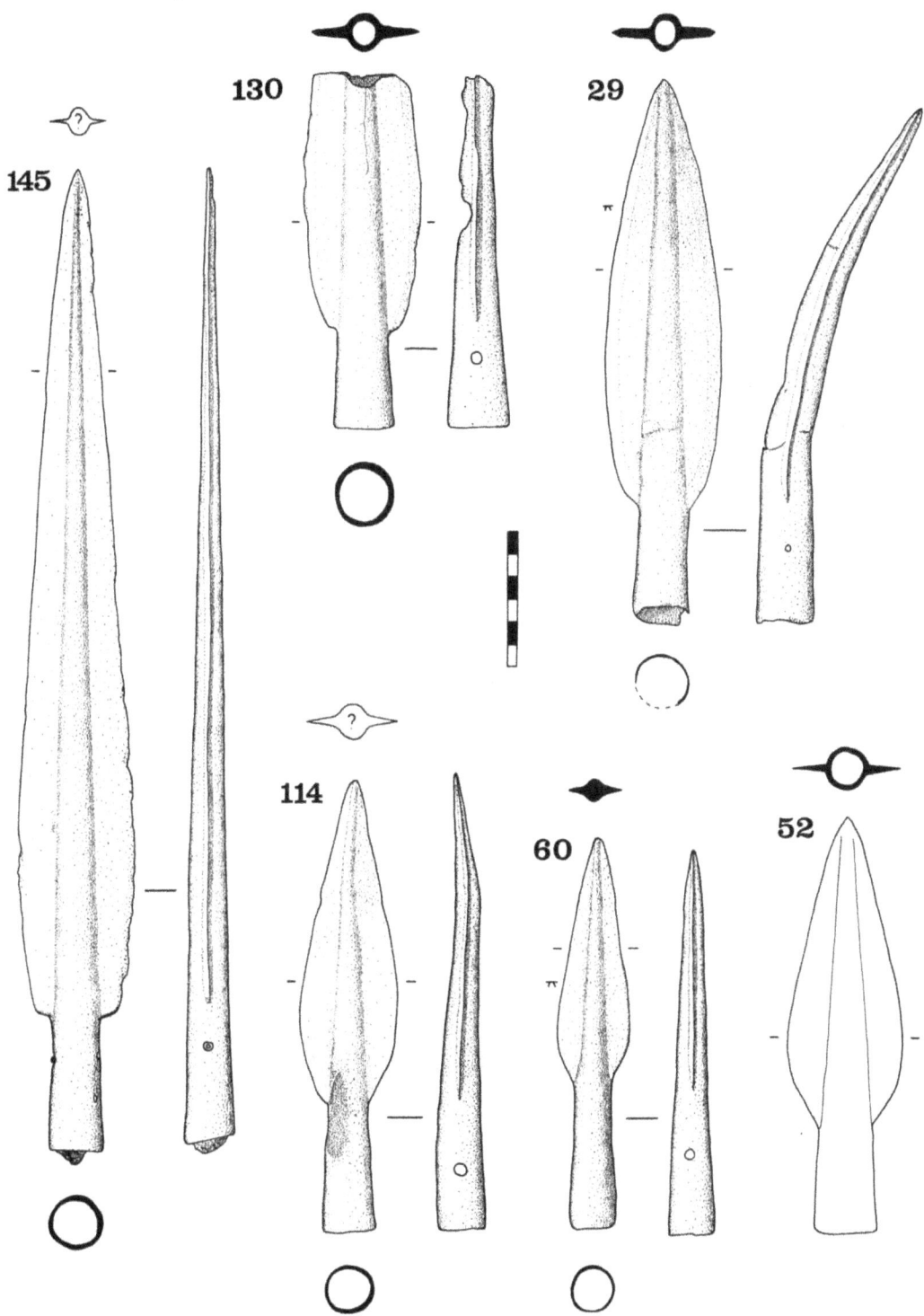

Fig. 19　Pegged Leaf-Shaped Spearheads

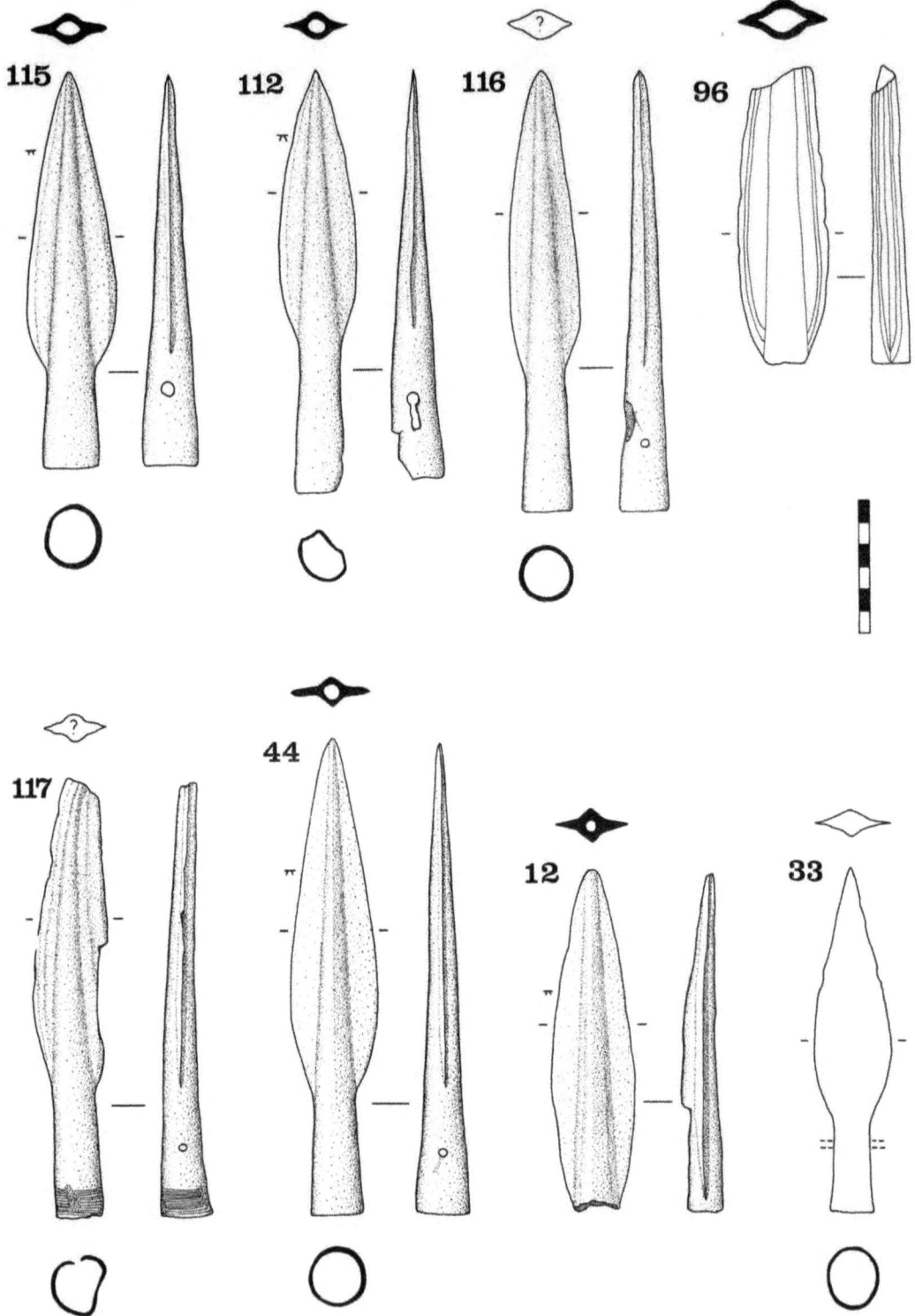

Fig. 20 Pegged Leaf-Shaped Spearheads

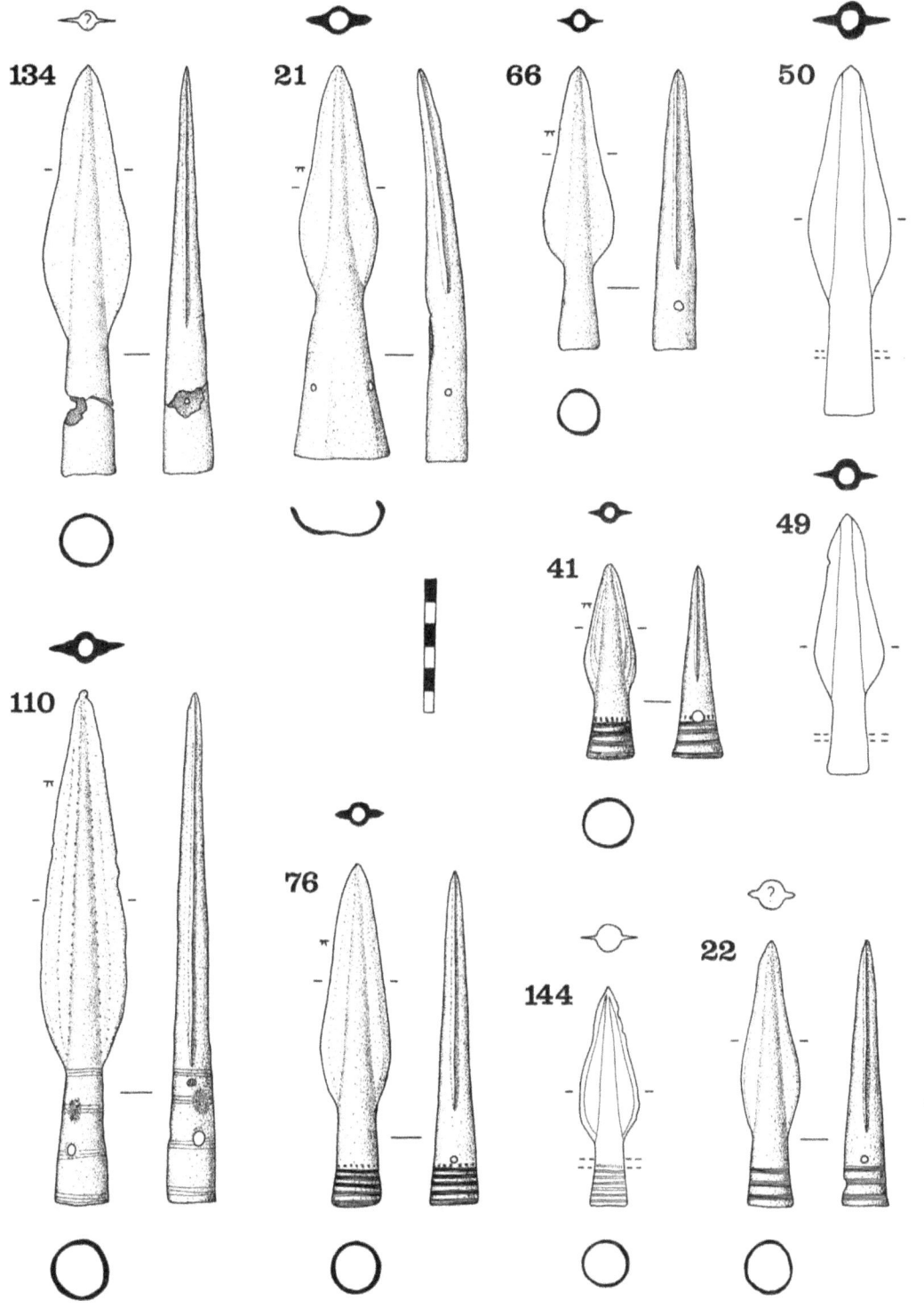

Fig. 21 Pegged Leaf-Shaped Spearheads

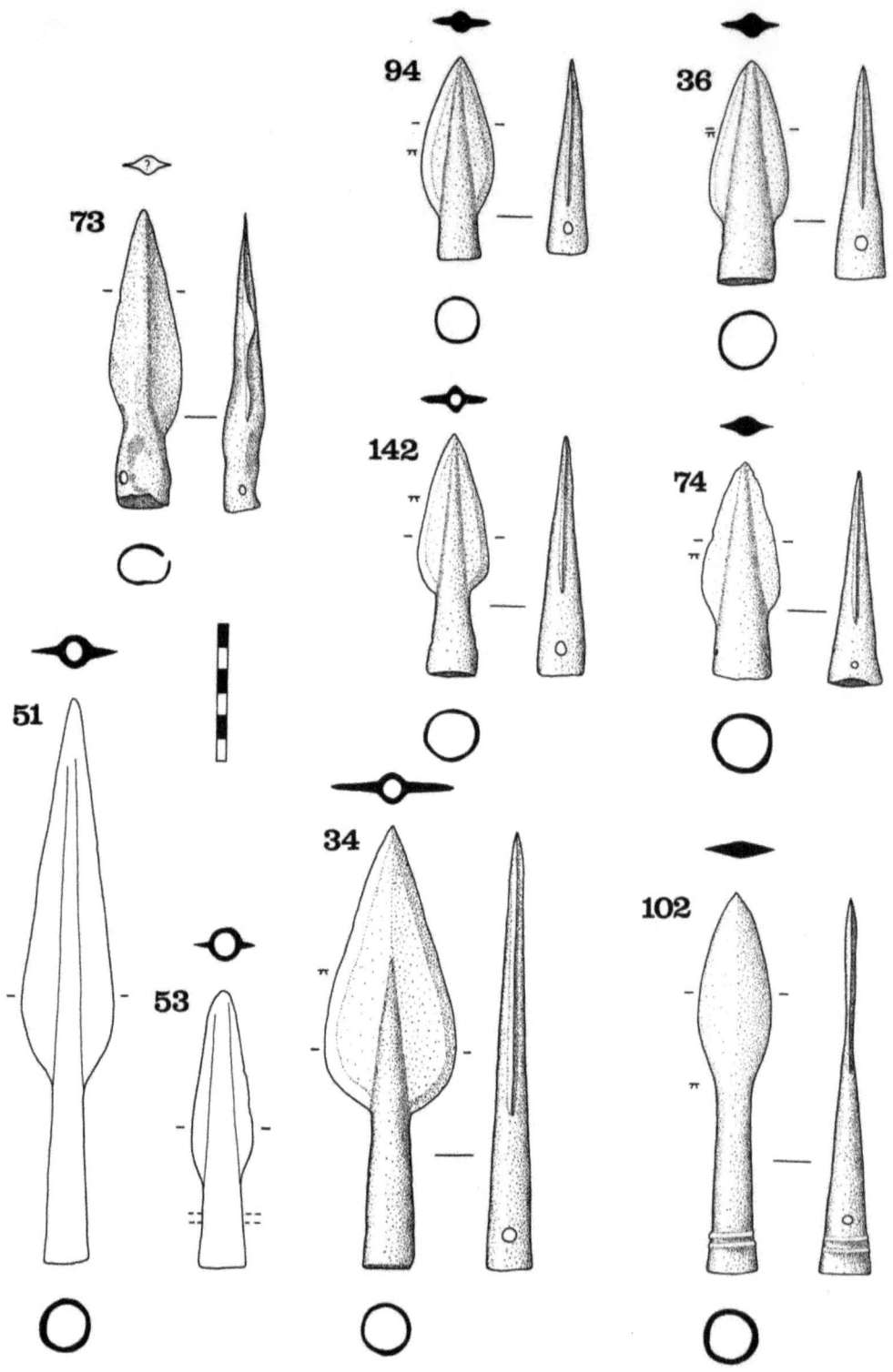

Fig. 22 Pegged Leaf-Shaped Spearheads

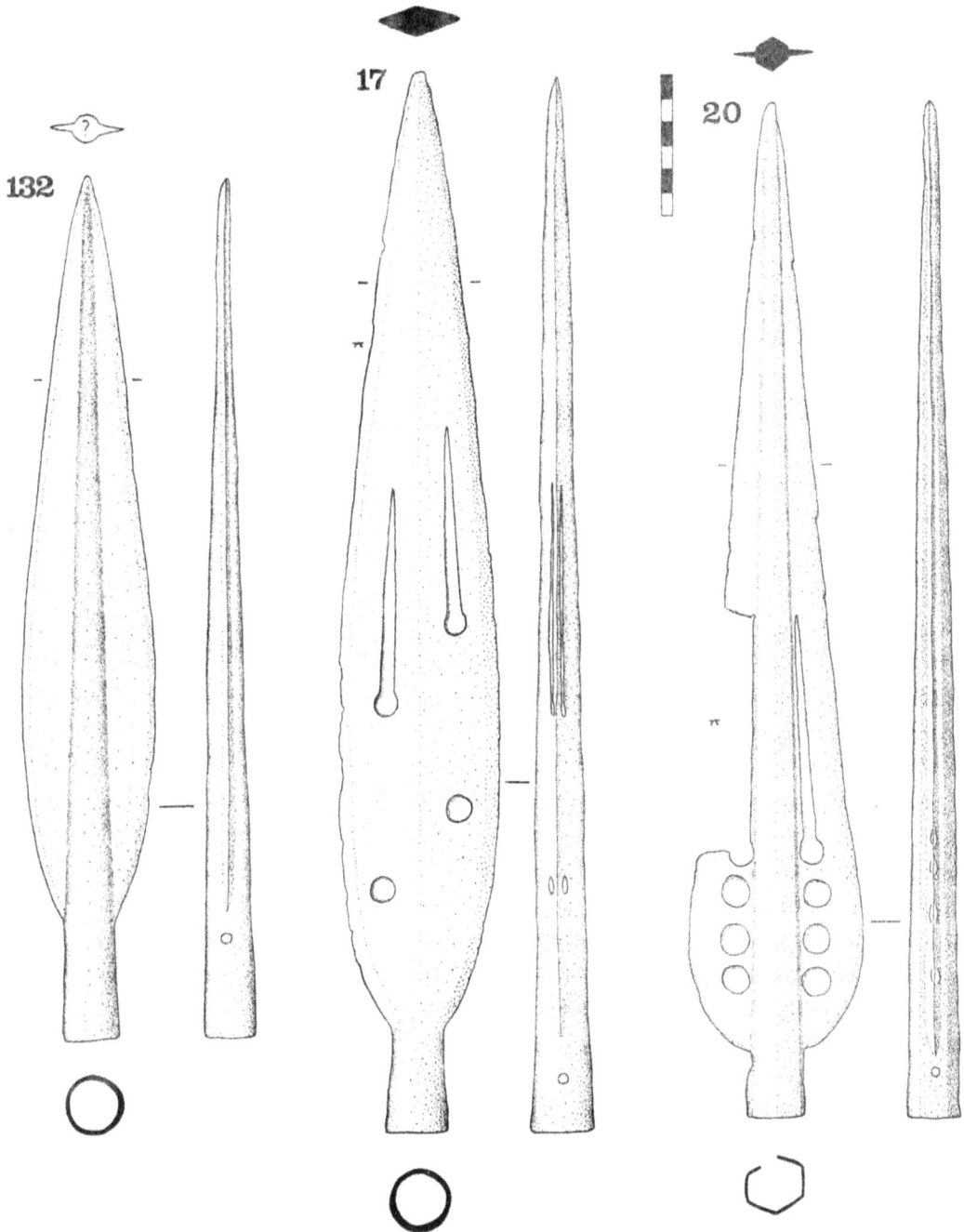

Fig. 23 Pegged Leaf-Shaped Spearheads

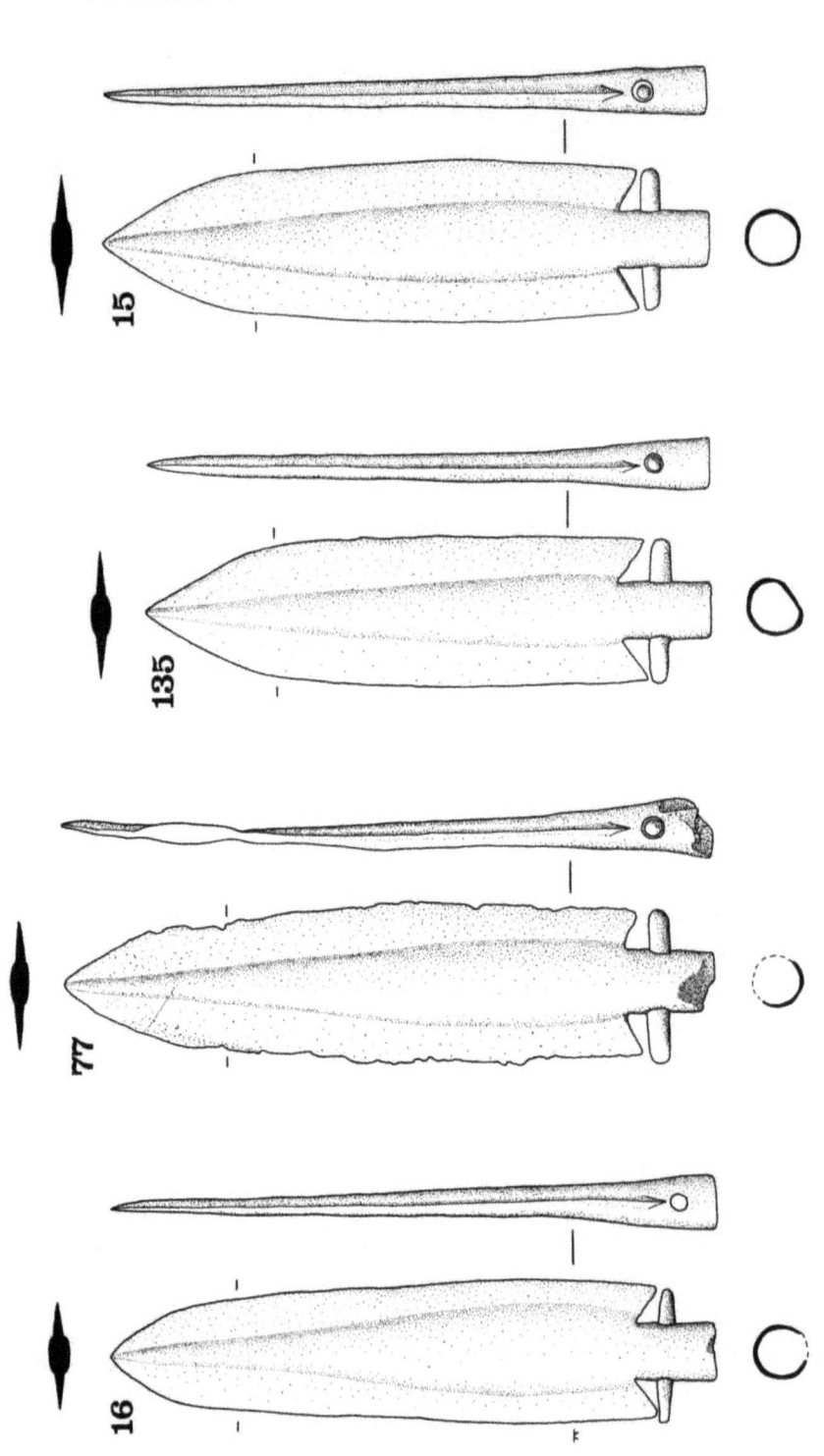

Fig. 24 Barbed Spearheads

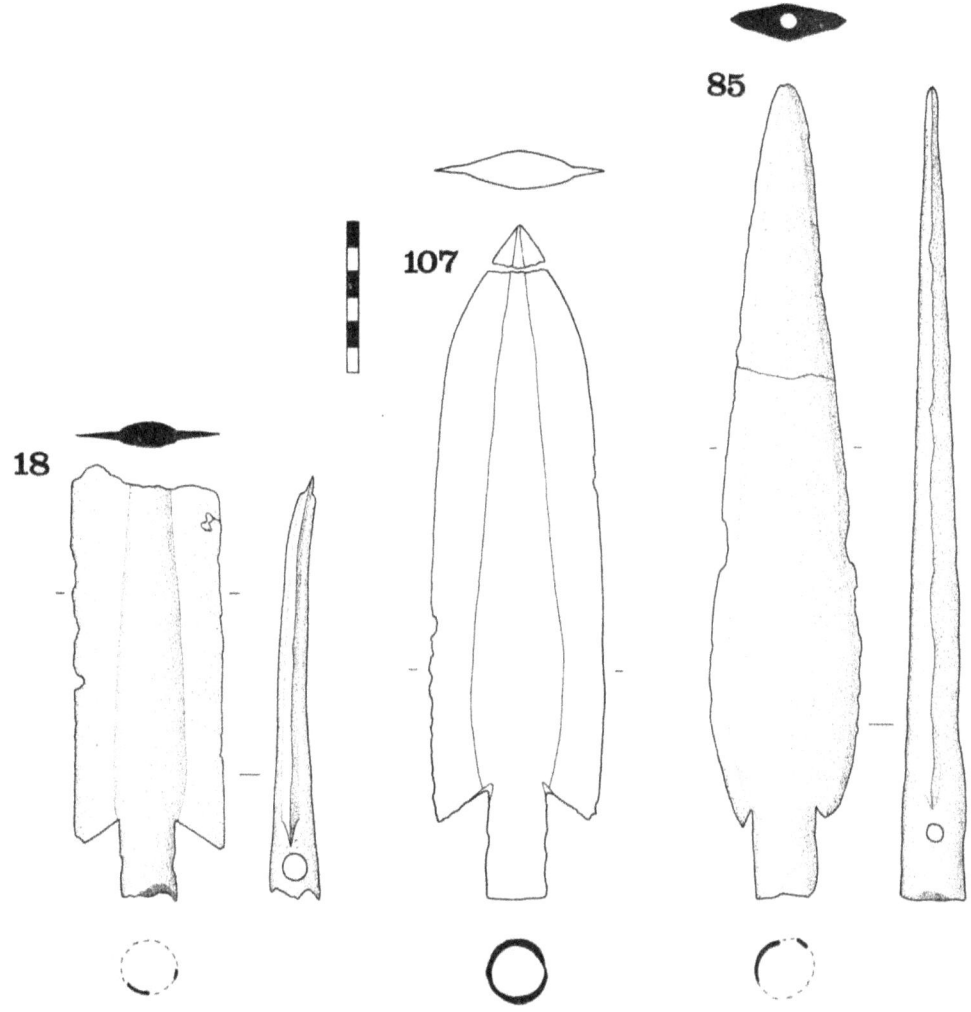

Fig. 25 Barbed Spearheads

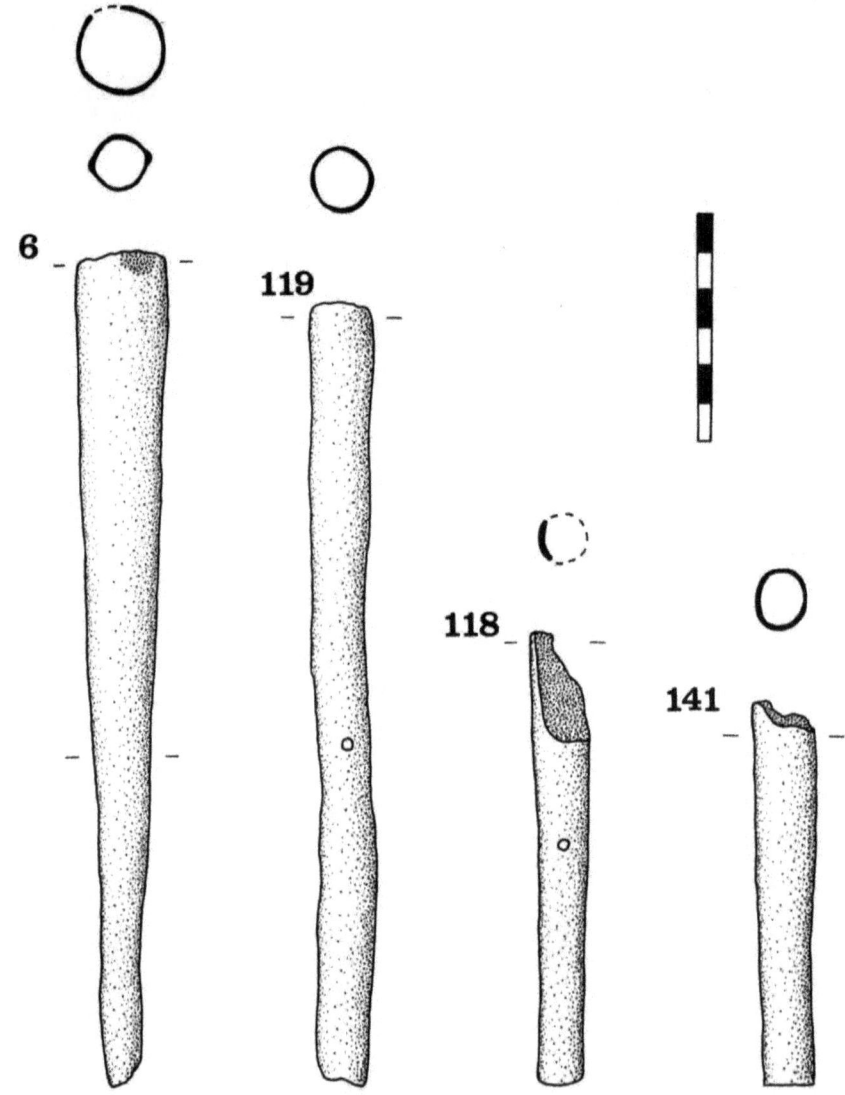

Fig. 26   Ferrules

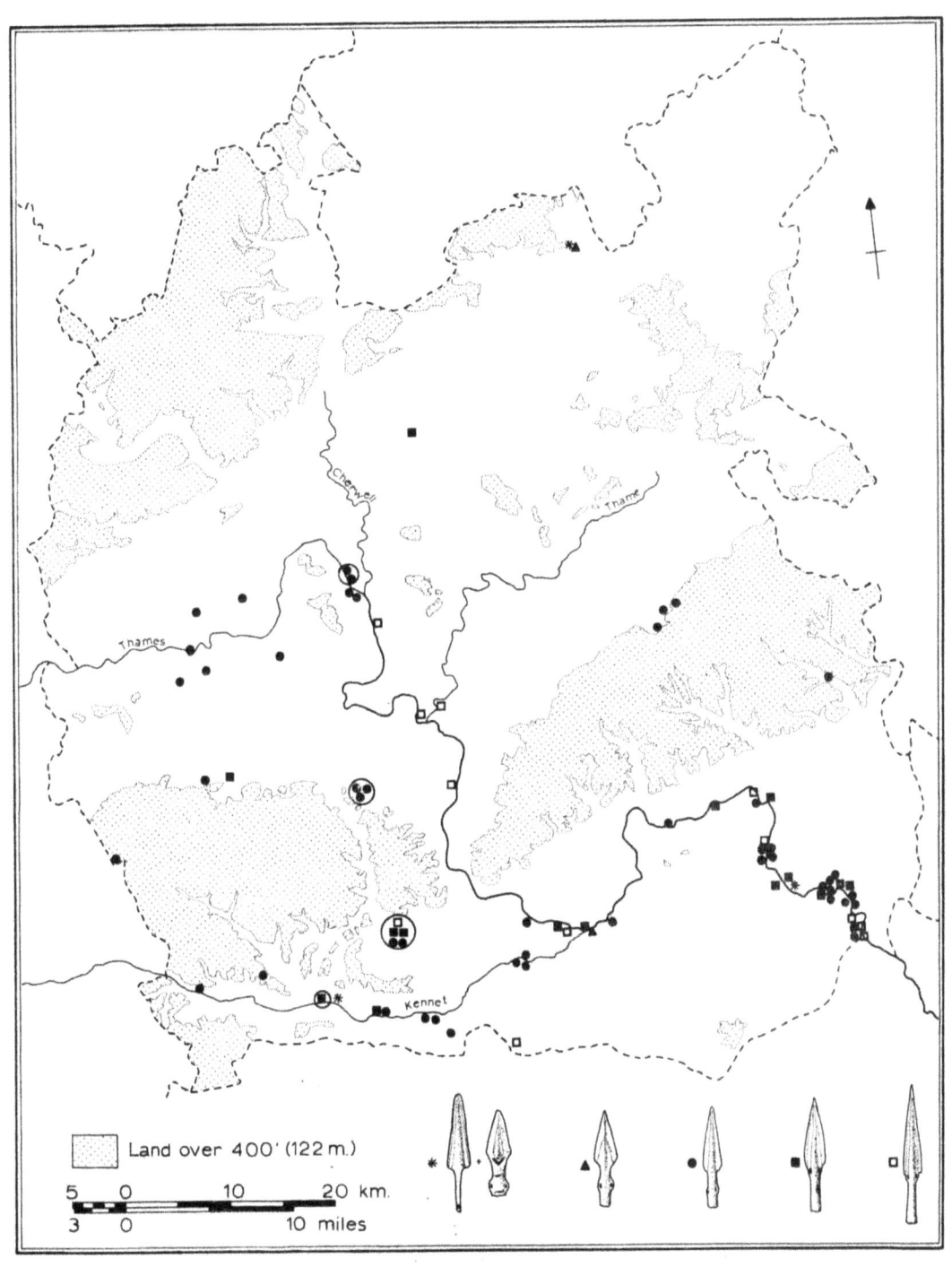

Fig. 27 The Distribution of EBA and Looped Spearheads

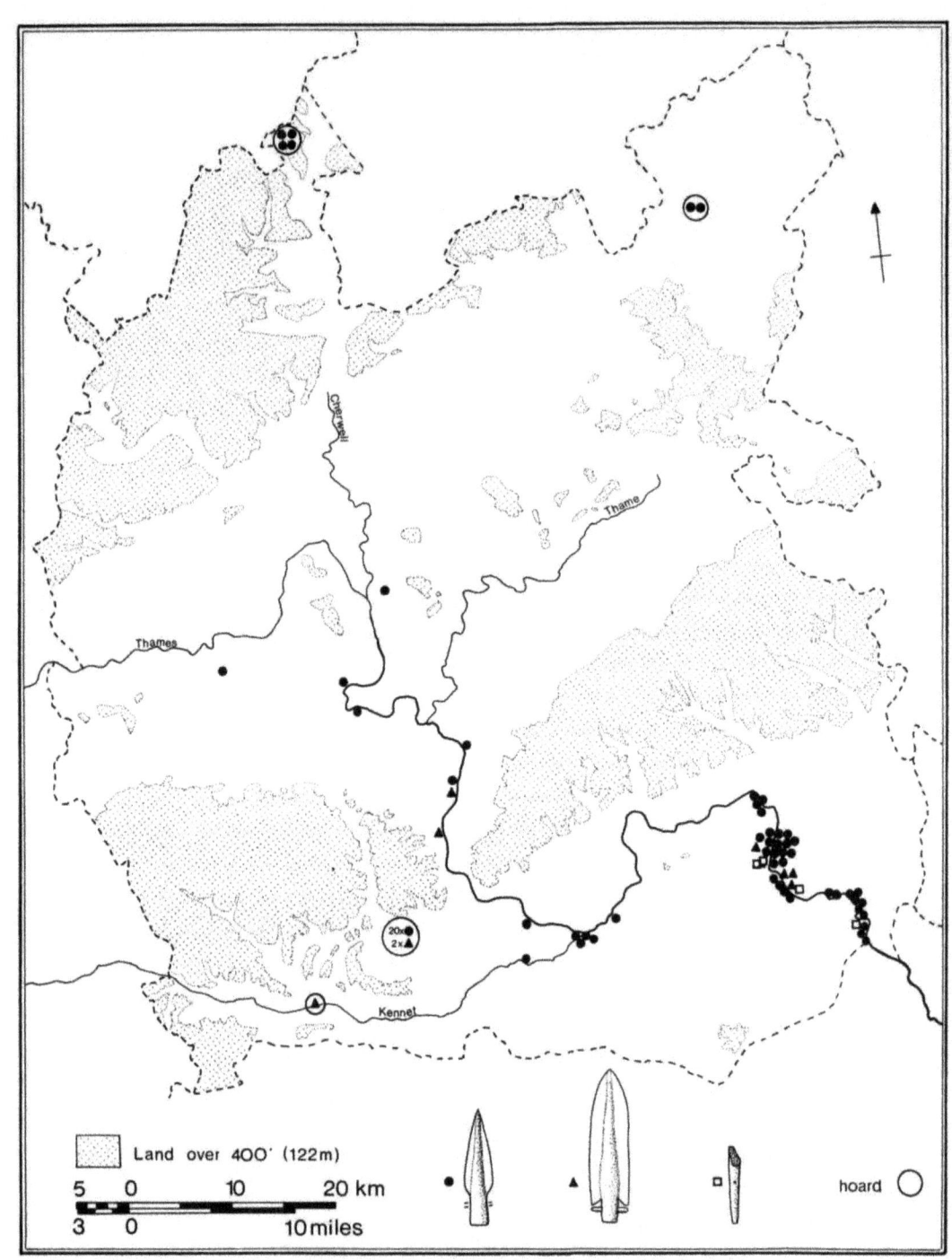

Fig. 28 The Distribution of Pegged Spearheads and Ferrules

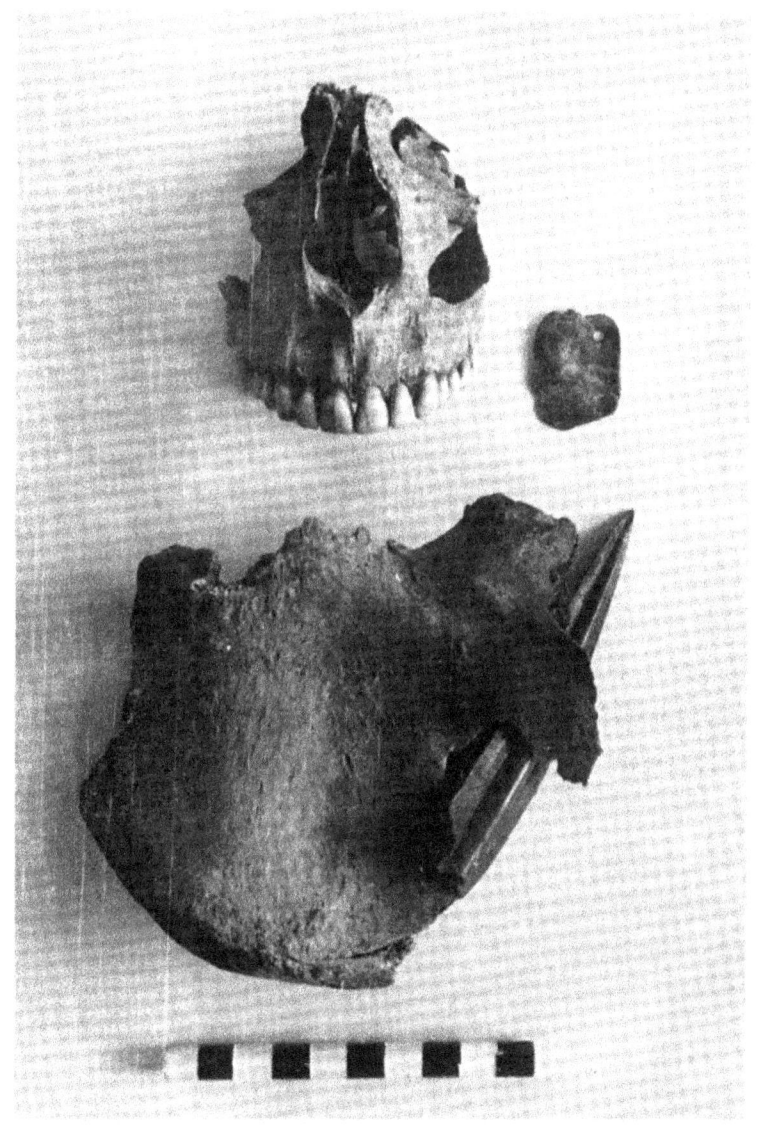

Plate 1

Spearhead from Dorchester (54), with Associated Finds

www.ingramcontent.com/pod-product-compliance
Lightning Source LLC
Chambersburg PA
CBHW061544010526
44113CB00023B/2792

* 9 7 8 0 9 0 4 5 3 1 6 1 9 *